# Assembly Stories:
# Therapy For Numb Bums

By Chris Pearson

Editors: Guy Williamson, Julie Middleton

Proofreader: Samantha Bowles

## Dedication:

## For Laura and Eddie

# **I recommend you do not read this book**

Well, that's a strange thing to title the first part of a book. What I mean is that I believe stories are better told than read. All of these stories have been told in real life assemblies, but apart from a few donated to other teachers and heads they have not been read.

They are, however, stories which can be a last-minute assembly, straight from the book, or used to build a real showstopper.

I feel that assemblies can be a proper event and can be the highlight of a child's day or an uncomfortable (hence the numb bum reference), boring brief period of near torture. Having a captive audience is a real privilege and we owe it to our children to give them something memorable, and a darn good listen.

I always think if you are holding a book and reading, your performance will probably not be as good as if you were doing it free style.

So please **do** read the stories and then, if you have a chance and the time, make them your own. Personalise them with names from the staffroom or with current events. Maybe add a silly voice or two, and there are even some opportunities to dance and act if you are that way inclined.

I have created a summary for each story with a map which will help you remember the main parts of each story to make telling them easier.

Having said all of that, I have printed this in a pretty large font to make it easier to read!

There are some recurring themes and I recently noticed that 'The Birds and The Beasts' seems to have been born of an unconscious nod to Aesop, but I think it's different enough.

Some tales have a comedic element, but some are serious and hopefully have a degree of gravitas.

I was a teacher for 39 years and a head for about half of that time. I have been asked to write these down many times, so I thought, why not? I feel I am a storyteller rather than a writer, so forgive my clumsy prose. It has been fun committing them to print but not as much fun as it was preforming them.

I hope you can build meaningful, enjoyable and memorable assemblies for your children and that **you** enjoy the stories, because if you don't, it's unlikely the kids will.

# The Stories

Four Desperate Animals

Acti and the Fly

Two Best Friends

The Unhappy Birds

The Useless Grasshopper

The Prince, his Friend and the Precious Vase

The Most Generous Person in Town

Making Alice Better

The Wisest Princess

The Crossroads

The Curious Rabbit

The Javelin

A Matter of Pride

Greedy Town

Derek and the Optimist

The Strangely Strong Weakling

The Creature in the Shell

The Genius Glasses

The Unhappy Prince

Trouble with the Birds and the Beasts

Three Farmers

# Story Notes

Here are some notes which will give you an idea about each story and the themes they cover. The notes are just a rough guide. The best thing to do is read the story and adapt it to your needs.

## 1. Four Desperate Animals

KS1 & KS2 (could be used for EY with some simplification)

This story tells of four animals who each have a problem which seems impossible to solve. They are in their own purgatory until a raven points out that each of them can solve one of the other's problems. They all help each other and there is a happy ending.

The themes are:

- Think problems through.
- Look at all the resources available.
- Help each other and cooperate using your skill set.

## 2. Acti and The Fly

KS1 & KS2

A baboon is the leader of his troop. He is strong and powerful, but when he upsets a fly, he cannot stop it pestering him. He is forced to realise that just being strong and powerful does not mean you can control things. You sometimes need to look more closely at yourself to solve problems.

The themes are:

- Brute strength does not solve all problems.
- Sometimes you need advice.
- You must look at the problem closely to find a solution.
- Self-control is a great strength.


## 3. Two Best Friends

KS1 & KS2

The story of two friends who have fallen on hard times. When one friend lets the other down, they look at their relationship and explore what being a real friend means.

The themes are:

- The responsibilities we have to our friends.
- Relationships are two-way things.
- Forgiveness is part of friendship.

## 4. The Unhappy Birds

EY (with some adaptation) KS1 & KS2

Three miserable birds are all very down about their failings, each being unhappy about the qualities they don't have. After a real moan, they are helped to see their good points by a passing eagle.

The themes are:

- We should look for positives rather than concentrating on negatives.
- We sometimes need help to see our good points.
- Individuals have different good points even when they share weaknesses.

## 5. The Useless Grasshopper

EY (with some editing) KS1 & KS2

The story of a grasshopper egg, which hatches not knowing what sort of animal it is. She finds out what she is but it is a tremendous disappointment because she cannot jump. She does not realise that over time things can change.

The themes are:

- It is important to know who you are.
- You should not give up on yourself.
- You do not know when you will reach your full potential.

## 6. The Prince, his Friend and the Precious Vase

KS1 & KS1 (Possibly EY with some adaptations)

The prince seems to have everything but is lonely and wants a friend. When he is allowed to go to school rather than have tutors, he hopes he will find a friend. When he does, he is happier but eventually needs to decide if his friendship is worth more than his pride.

The themes are:

- Friends are important.
- You cannot put a value on a good friend.
- Sometimes your pride stops you from making good decisions.

## 7. The Most Generous Person

KS1 & KS2

In a town where people are only bothered about what they have, the mayor launches a competition to find the most generous person. The results surprise everyone, but the town becomes a better place.

The themes are:

- Being overly competitive can be a bad thing.
- Being generous has to be a thoughtful act.
- You can give more than money.
- You don't have to be rich to make a difference.

## 8. Making Alice Better

KS2 (KS1 with some additional explanations)

The story of a young squirrel who is feeling low. She wants to change things. She tries to be things she is not and puts herself in danger. The message is to appreciate yourself for the good things about you. The only thing to change sometimes is the way you see yourself.

The themes are:

- Look for the positives in yourself.
- Don't try to be what you are not.
- Sometimes you need to just accept who you are.


## 9. The Wisest Princess

KS1 & KS2

The Queen wants to know which of her daughters will make the best queen when she steps down. She gives them a test, and each Princess reacts differently, which shows the Queen who should be the next monarch.

The themes are:

- You need to think about everyone.
- People can work together for the greater good.
- It is better for everyone to be OK rather than some rich and some poor.

## 10. The Crossroads

KS2 (Possibly KS1 with some explanations)

Three travellers all reach a crossroads at the edge of town and are all in some distress. A wise old man helps each of them to solve their problems by explaining the actual causes of their anxieties.

The themes are:

- Although problems might seem the same, they can be very different.
- Sometimes you need someone else to help you understand your problems.
- You need to deal with problems, not run from them.


## 11. The Curious Rabbit

EY, KS1 &KS2

The story of a young rabbit who wants to know where rainbows end and is determined to find out. Although he never solves this problem, his curiosity results in him finding lots of other things which none of the other rabbits knew before.

The themes are:

- It is good to follow your dreams.
- Being curious leads to discoveries.
- We need curious people to make discoveries.
- There are more ways to succeed than we sometimes think.

## 12. The Javelin

KS1 & KS2

Xandro will do anything to avoid PE and sport in general. He does not want to be teased by others and always has an excuse. When he has a go when no-one is looking, he realises that you don't know how good you are unless you try.

The themes are:

- You don't know how good you are until you give it a go.
- You shouldn't worry about failing.
- You can surprise yourself if you try.


## 13. A Matter of Pride

KS1 & KS2 (could be used for EY with some simplification)

This is the story of a girl who is asked to speak to her class about something of which she is proud. Whilst others talk about what they have or have done, she talks about where she is from, her heritage and her family.

The themes are:

- How precious families are.
- Being proud of heritage and family history.
- The true value of who you are.

## 14. Greedy Town

KS1 & KS2

The story of a town where the possessions you own are a measure of your worth as a person and where people want to show off how rich they are. This helps a gang of armed robbers to trick them and steal their possessions, except one man who is new and whose most treasured possessions are photos of his family.

The themes are:

- Greed can consume you.
- There are more important things than wealth.
- Memories are precious.


## 15. Derek and the Optimist

KS1 & KS2

This is the tale of Derek, a miserable caterpillar who does not know what lies ahead, and his friend who keeps telling him that things will be ok, and you never know when things might get better, and eventually they do.

The themes are:

- Keep positive.
- You never know what lies ahead.
- Things can change.

## 16. The Strangely Strong Weakling

EY (with some explaining) KS1 & KS2

When a strange new animal arrives in the jungle, she shows the other animals that if you play to your strengths, you can stand up to those who try to use aggression and threats to push you around.

The themes are:

- Don't let others push you around.
- There are strengths other than muscles.
- You might not know what you are dealing with.
- Think of your own strengths and use them.


## 17. The Creature in the Shell

EY (with simplification and maybe props), KS1 & KS2

This is a story about trying to get a little animal out of its shell. Some big, silly men try to scare, shake and just demand it out, whilst the little girl, who has been watching, shows that giving the creature a reason to come out and a sense of security is much more effective.

The themes are:

- Winning someone over is more effective than forcing them.
- Being threatening might not get you what you want.
- Being aggressive can make you seem silly.

## 18. The Genius Glasses

KS1 & KS2

In this story, a miserable and angry Queen is tricked into looking for good rather than bad by a couple of teenagers who want their kingdom to be a happier place. They are inspired by the 'Emperor's new clothes' story and they make the place better for everyone.

The themes are:

- Miserable leaders make miserable places.
- If you look for positives, you will find them.
- Vanity makes you easy to trick.


## 19. The Unhappy Prince

KS1 & KS2 (could be used for EY with some simplification)

This is a story about a lucky, rich prince who too readily feels sorry for himself. He thinks the world is against him and does not realise that other people have much more serious problems and difficult lives.

The themes are:

- Be grateful for what you have.
- Appreciate other people's situations.
- Learn from experience.

## 20. Trouble with the Birds and the Beasts

EY, KS1 & KS2

A bat gets blown off course and is treated differently by groups depending on whether they think she is a bird or a beast. The bat learns an important lesson about judging others.

The themes are:

- It is foolish to judge someone or something by the group to which they belong.
- Individuals act differently when a group puts pressure on each other.
- It is better to judge by who someone is rather than who we think they are.


## 21. Three Farmers

KS1 & KS2

Three farming sisters, who are all different, inherit a farm from their mother. The hardest working sister learns that because she was angry with one of her sisters, she let that change the way she behaved, and that is not a good thing.

The themes are:

- Working together is important.
- Anger can make us behave poorly.
- Don't let the way others behave change how you behave.
- Helping others is a good thing to do.
- Forgiveness is an important quality.

# Four Desperate Animals

The clearing was quiet. The wind gently tickled the trees, and their laughter was the only noise. Apart from the tiny voice of a mouse who was scurrying around in circles repeating, "Oh dear, oh dear me, oh dear." It didn't seem to have any real purpose, it just kept running round and round and round.

Meanwhile, on a path a short distance from the clearing, a horse had just been bitten by a fly, a horsefly as it happens. The bite was just at the base of his neck and between his shoulders. It itched, it itched very much indeed, and the horse needed to scratch it. He rubbed against a tree; it didn't work. He rubbed against a rock; it didn't work. He even rolled on his back; it did not work.

"Arrrggghh!" shouted the horse. "Oh dear, oh dear, oh dear." The horse did a double kick and twisted its long neck. The itch was driving him mad. "It's driving me mad!" he shouted and galloped along the path towards the clearing.

High in the sky was a very happy magpie. She was happy because in her mouth was a bright, shiny silver earring, which she had found. A human had obviously dropped it. It's well-known that magpies like shiny things and this earring was perfect. She was heading back to her nest, and she was very, very pleased. So delighted, in fact that she couldn't stop herself from cawing out loud with happiness. She just couldn't help herself. She, rather dimly, opened her mouth and cawed a loud gritty caw. Of course, this was not a bright thing to do as the lovely, shiny silver earring slipped from her beak and fell down, down, down to the wood below. The magpie's happiness turned to despair. "Oh dear, oh dear," she called, "Oh dear."

The earring landed in the clearing. It bounced, rolled and disappeared down a crack in the dry earth.

The horse arrived in the clearing, dancing and kicking and rubbing on anything he could see. He could not get to the itch, and it was driving him MAD! The magpie swooped down into the clearing desperately searching for her earring. The mouse was still running round and round for no apparent reason. They were all saying, "Oh dear, oh dear, oh dear!"

Another sound joined that of the giggling leaves and the three anxious animals. It was the sound of panting, exhausted panting. A rabbit stumbled into the clearing, gasping for breath. He could hardly walk and was finding merely standing quite an effort. He managed to get into the middle of the clearing and then he collapsed in a heap. His chest was pounding up and down as he struggled to get his breath. "Oh dear… oh dear… dear, dear me."

The horse noticed the rabbit and although his back was still itching like crazy, he went across and asked the exhausted rodent, "What's the matter with you?"

"Oh dear, oh dear," the rabbit panted. "I'm late, very, very late."

"Have you been running?" the horse enquired.

"Yes, running so far, I'm so late. I can't go on, oh dear, dear me!"

"Well, that's a shame but you're lucky, at least you will not go mad. I have a fly bite which is just driving me MAD!" and with that he charged off to try to rub his back on a tree.

Meanwhile, the magpie had found the earring. Found it but couldn't get to it. The shiny treasure had settled down in the crack. However, it was too deep for the magpie to reach with her beak. She kept ramming her head down, banging away, but was well short of her target. The horse and the rabbit watched the slightly bonkers bird and after a while told her to stop and that she would never reach it. The magpie stopped and hopped over. "What's the matter with you two?" she asked.

"I have a dreadful itch," said the horse through gritted teeth. "And it's driving me MAD!" He ran over to a big rock and tried to rub against it.

"And I'm dreadfully late," puffed and wheezed the rabbit, "and if it's too late before I get home, the foxes will be out, and you know what foxes do to rabbits." The rabbit made a throat-cutting action with his front paw, "but I am just too tired to keep running. Oh, dear!"

"Oh dear," said the magpie, "dear, dear me. What about her?" she said, pointing at the mouse who was still running round, although she was getting slower by now.

"Oi!" the horse shouted towards the mouse. "Why are you running round and round like that?" The magpie, horse and rabbit made their way towards the mouse. "Well?" asked the horse when they got there.

The mouse lifted its tired head, "I'm lost!"

"Oh," said the rabbit.

"I fell out of my nest and think I bumped my head. Now I seem to have wandered away, but I can't remember where my nest is. I know it's next to a tree stump and opposite a farm gate, but when you are as little as me it's very hard because all you can really see is grass… Oh dear, oh dear oh dear."

So, there it was, four desperate animals; the horse with his itch, the rabbit who very late but was too tired to move, the magpie staring down a crack in the earth at a beautiful earring which she couldn't reach and a mouse running in circles looking for his house which he knew wasn't there. All of them saying "Oh dear, oh dear, oh dear."

After a short while, the crow arrived. The crow was a cousin of the magpie but was much, much cleverer. She watched the four desperate animals for a while from a low branch in a tree and then shouted across, "Excuse me! Excuse me, please."

They stopped what they were doing and the rabbit, who had got his breath back a little, called back, "Yes, what do you want?"

"I just was wondering what was happening. You look a strange bunch, one of you rubbing on things, one of you running round in circles, one staring down a crack in the earth and one on the ground panting."

The horse explained what the matter was, and the crow listened as he told her about each animal's desperate situation. At the end the crow thought and then said, "I see, I see."

"Well, of course you see," snapped the angry, exhausted rabbit, "the horse has just told you."

"No, I see what the problem is."

"What do you mean *THE* problem? I just told you we have four problems," said the horse, he was also getting angry, and his back was really, really itching.

"No, no," the crow insisted, "you just have one problem."

"We have a problem each," said the tired mouse, who had finally given up running round in circles.

"No, just one problem," the crow repeated. "Shall I tell you what it is?"

"OK," the magpie answered. "If it helps me get my earring back."

"It will," said the crow. "THE problem is that you are all being a bit dim!"

The four animals were very unhappy at being called dim. "How rude!" said the mouse.

"You can't speak to us like that," the angry rabbit snarled.

"What a nerve!" the horse gasped.

"That's very unkind," the magpie sounded hurt.

"Oh, I'm sorry," the crow said. "I was a bit rude I guess, but you really are being a bit dim. Let me explain. You all have a problem and a problem that you cannot solve. However, if you were to think about each other's problems, then maybe things would be different."

"I can't think of anything apart from my horrid itch. It's driving me MAD!"

"I know," the crow actually sounded sympathetic, "and you can't get to it can you? What you need is someone who is nimble and has little claws which could really give that itch a good old scratch. How does that sound?"

"Oh, that sounds wonderful, I'd give anything for that, anything!" The horse had tears in his eyes at the thought.

"Well, look around. Can you see anyone who might help?" The crow was looking straight at the mouse.

"The mouse is perfect!" the horse shouted with delight.

He lowered his head, and the mouse quickly climbed onto his mane and down to the base of his neck where the fly bite was, all red and round. She quickly got to work, her sharp little claws scratching just on the spot that the horse had failed to scratch for the past hour. "AAAAAWWWWWWW YESSSSSS!" The horse's relief was like an avalanche of loveliness. "That is perfect!"

"See," said the crow, feeling pleased with herself.

"But I can't help the mouse find her house," the horse said glumly. "I wouldn't know where to start."

"No, I agree, but someone who could have a good look from a height would quickly spot a tree stump opposite a gate," the crow pointed out.

"I could have a look," said the magpie. "The mouse helped the horse; I could help the mouse."

"Exactly," said the crow.

The magpie flew high into the sky. "There it is," she cawed down. "I can see the tree stump and the gate. Haha." She was very pleased with herself. She landed next to mouse and explained that if she followed the second path and then turned right at the old wheelbarrow, she'd be home in no time at all.

"Oh good, thank you magpie, thank you crow," and off the happy mouse went to find her home.

"Well, that was good," the magpie smiled inside (it's hard to smile with a beak!). "But I still don't have my earring!" The internal smile disappeared.

"That's true," said the crow, trying to sound sad. "What you need is someone who is superb at digging. Maybe someone who digs holes to live in. Someone who really knows about digging."

"Well, who is that?" the magpie was fed up and not thinking, but fortunately the rabbit had been listening.

"Me! That's who that is. I live in a burrow which I dug myself. I could have that earring out of there in no time," and he did.

The magpie was soon grasping the shiny earring in her beak and taking off, feeling great again.

"Just you left with a problem now rabbit!" the crow said, looking across at the horse.

"I get it," said the horse. "Come on, get on," he said, lowering his neck.

The rabbit climbed up and made himself comfortable on the horse's back and off the horse galloped, getting the rabbit home in a couple of minutes, long before the foxes were out looking for their dinner. As the rabbit vanished down his rabbit hole, the crow landed in a tree nearby.

"See," the crow said, "see what you can do if you all work together."

# **FOUR DESPERATE ANIMALS**

This story tells of four animals who each have a problem which seems impossible to solve. They are in their own purgatory until a crow points out that each of them can solve one of the other's problems. They all help each other and there is a happy ending.

The themes are:

- Think problems through.
- Look at all the resources available.
- Help each other and cooperate using your skill set.

## Story map

- In a wood with a clearing.
- A horse is bitten at the base of its neck by a horsefly, and it itches terribly.
- A magpie drops a precious silver earring which hits the ground in a clearing and vanishes down a crack.
- A mouse is lost and cannot find her way home and runs round and round in circles.
- A rabbit is a long way from home and will not get home before the foxes come out.
- Four animals all with problems that they cannot solve. They are all panicking and saying " Oh dear, oh dear".
- The animals all show an interest in each other but are only really bothered about their own problem.
- All seem hopeless until a crow shows them that although they cannot solve their own problem, they can solve each other's.

- The mouse can scratch the horse's itch.
- The magpie can fly high to look for the mouse's home.
- The rabbit can dig the earring out of the ground.
- The horse can carry the exhausted rabbit home before the foxes come out to hunt.
- The animals realise that when we help each other we have more chance of solving problems.

# Acti and the Fly

Baboons are big, powerful apes. They live in troops with a leader and a strict order below that boss babboon, a bit like an army. The troop in this story had a leader called Acti, who was a proud and strong animal. He got angry very quickly and if anything, or anyone questioned his authority, he put them in their place, threatening them with his big teeth and scary muscles. The other members of the troop knew that it was very silly to argue with Acti.

One day, the troop were walking towards some rocks trying to find shade from the hot afternoon sun. Acti, of course, had to choose where to sit first. He spotted a place that he liked the look of. It had a high slab of rock which threw a cool shadow across a second flat rock. Acti moved over to the prize spot and lowered himself into the pool of shade. He did not see a horsefly (horseflies are big for flies but tiny compared to a baboon) who had also been resting in the shade. Suddenly the unsuspecting insect had Acti's big hairy bottom lowering towards her. The horsefly just managed to fly away as the ape settled down. Acti was completely unaware of the fly, but the fly was now very angry. She didn't appreciate being made to move and now she planned her revenge.

She waited until Acti looked comfortable and then went and buzzed around the baboon's head, really annoying him. He waved his arms around, not having a chance of ever hitting her. Then, when Acti was wound up, the fly landed on him, right in the middle of his forehead. Without thinking, the great ape swung his huge right arm towards the fly with all his power. Now, it's important to know that flies have very quick reactions, and the insect saw the hand coming, so she could easily fly away before it arrived. Smack! The hand hit, not the fly but Acti's own head. "Urghhh!" yelled Acti as the force of his own slap knocked him off his rock. He rolled down onto the dusty ground with a thump.

"Did Acti just punch himself in the head?" one of the younger baboons asked another.

"I think so," said the other baboon, "but say nothing, he'll go mad if he thinks we saw!"

Acti was furious and embarrassed and quickly went back up to the rock as if nothing had happened.

The fly was so happy. She thought it was the funniest thing she had ever seen. She thought, "Well, if it was fun first time I wonder if the silly big ape will fall for it again." She waited until Acti had settled and then started to buzz around his head for a second time. Acti waved his arms around again. The fly dodged away from them easily. She would move away, then come back to annoy the troop leader. And gosh, was he annoyed? When she thought Acti was angry enough, she landed right on his forehead in the same place as before. She so hoped that he would fall for it again, and he did. As soon as she landed, his huge hand came hurtling towards her. She waited until it was moving quickly then hopped up into the air and the thwack of Acti's hand on his own head sounded loud around the peaceful rocks, making all the other baboons look up, in time to see their chief tumble down into the dust.

"I think he has done it again," said the first young baboon.

"I know," said the second, "I'm trying not to laugh."

Acti was even more angry and embarrassed. The fly was even more happy. She thought it was fantastic!

The next day, the troop was eating fruit in some tall, shady trees, which were gently swaying in the light breeze. They were high in the branches, with Acti having the first choice of where to sit, of course. All was calm, and the baboons were having a lovely time, when who should fly by but the horsefly. As soon as she saw Acti high in the tree, she couldn't stop herself. She flew straight up to the treetops and started buzzing around the big ape. He instantly knew it was the same fly as the day before, which made him angry and lose his temper immediately. His fury made him stop thinking and start reacting. The moment the fly landed on his head, he swung his big hand at it and of course, the fly flew, the hand hit, and the huge baboon tumbled through the branches and crashed onto the ground below.

"He has done it again!" the young baboon said to his friend. "Do you think he is ill? He doesn't usually punch himself in the head and fall off things."

"No, he doesn't. Should we ask him?" the second young ape asked.

"No way. I'm not going to talk to him about it. He'll go mad."

"No, fair enough. Probably quite right," the second ape agreed.

The next day, the same thing happened again. This time the troop was just sitting in the long grass resting when the fly spotted a chance for her to play her new favourite game. She buzzed around Acti's head and sure enough, before long, the great leader was throwing his arms around and then punching himself in the face. This time the whole troop saw, and all pretended they didn't.

The young baboons thought it was all most strange. They dared not talk to Acti about it, but they spoke with Hugo, who was an ancient and wise baboon. He would know what to do. It surprised Hugo to hear about Acti's behaviour. He had never heard of such a thing before. He told the two young baboons that he would observe Acti to see if he could find the trouble.

The next day nothing happened, but the day after that the horsefly spotted the troop sitting by the river. She thought," Oh what fun". She flew over, wound up Acti, and soon he punched himself in the head. Just like the other times, only this time Hugo was watching. He saw exactly what happened and thought it was funny. Acti did not, he was absolutely furious. He was not used to not being in control, because he was the strongest and the toughest, and in his world, the strongest and the toughest were in charge and could do what they wanted.

A little while later, as the sun was going down, Hugo went up to Acti for a chat, as he sometimes did. "Are you OK, Acti? You look troubled."

Usually, Acti would have said that he was fine. He never wanted to appear weak in front of the other baboons, but this was not a usual time.

"No, I'm not OK." He spoke in a hushed voice. He could talk to Hugo but didn't want the others to hear. "It's this fly. It's making my life a misery. It seems to follow me. I can't do anything about it. It is spoiling my life. I don't know what to do, Hugo."

Hugo could tell how desperate the leader was. So, he thought he could speak honestly. "Acti, you are a strong, powerful and great baboon. You rule this troop with your strength and power. No baboon in the troop will challenge you because they know that you are the strongest and toughest."

Acti enjoyed hearing these things and felt a bit better. "But," continued Hugo, "you have a weakness."

"What! "growled Acti, "I am the strongest, toughest ape in this entire jungle."

"Yes, of course you are, but strengths and weaknesses have many forms. Your weakness is nothing to do with your muscles. Your weakness is that you get angry. You lose your temper and when we lose our temper, we lose control. If you keep control, you can manage the situation," the old baboon said wisely, and with a little fear.

Acti realised that he did have a bad temper but could not see a way of beating the fly. "But the fly gets me so angry!" he snarled.

"And makes you punch yourself in the head," the old baboon managed not to laugh.

Acti was embarrassed. "Yes, but I get so cross and annoyed." His voice getting louder.

"And the fly laughs at you. It has won, and you, big, strong, powerful Acti, have lost," Hugo said, rather bravely.

"But how can I win?!" Acti was getting wound up again.

"Stay calm. The fly is winding you up. I imagine just for fun. You must remain calm. Win by stopping the fly winning."

Acti knew that would be very difficult, but also knew that Hugo was right.

The next day the troop was eating some soft fruit from trees near the lake. All was calm, the lake was like a pool of silver and the trees were gently swaying in the light breeze. Then guess who flew by. The fly spotted her old friend Acti and was soon buzzing around the great ape's head. Acti instantly wanted to attack back and was about to wave his enormous hands around, but then thought about Hugo's words. He thought, "Stay calm, don't get wound up". He ignored the buzzing of the horsefly. Even when she landed on his head, he allowed her to crawl around. He desperately wanted to crush the fly but kept reminding himself to stay calm. The fly was very disappointed and after a few minutes got bored and flew away. Acti felt a wave of happiness and success wash over him as he heard the fly buzzing away. He felt so good, better than he had felt for a long time.

The following day the troop were lazing down by the river. The fly was once again buzzing about. She had been miserable at her failure to wind Acti up the previous day but thought she would have another go at annoying the big, powerful ape. She buzzed around his head; she buzzed behind him, in front of him and even landed on the end of his nose so that the troop leader could see her. He so wanted to grab her and squash her, but he remembered Hugo and how good he had felt the day before when he had beaten the fly, so he did nothing. Soon the fly became bored and flew away thinking, "My fun has ended here, I shall go somewhere else." Acti clenched his fist in triumph.

A few days later, Hugo went up to Acti and asked how things were. "Things are fine," said the big baboon. "I have had many fights that I have won with my strength and power but staying in control and refusing to let the fly win has been my greatest victory, because I won by overcoming my weakness."

# ACTI AND THE FLY

A baboon is the leader of his troop. He is strong and powerful, but when he upsets a fly, he cannot stop it pestering him. He is forced to realise that just being strong and powerful does not mean you can control everything. You sometimes need to look more closely at yourself to solve problems.

The themes are:

- Brute strength does not solve all problems.
- Sometimes you need advice.
- You must look at the problem closely to find a solution.
- Self-control is a great strength.

## Story map

- Acti is the powerful and scary leader of a troop of baboons.
- All the other baboons fear Acti.
- Acti nearly sits on a fly when looking for some shade, and the fly gets angry.
- The fly decides to get even by annoying Acti.
- She repeatedly flies round his head, even landing on his nose. Each time Acti tries to hit the fly, she flies off and he punches himself in the face, making him fall out of the tree or from the rock he is sitting on. The fly thinks that this is hilarious.
- Every day the fly torments the big ape and every day he ends up hitting himself in the face.
- Two young baboons see Acti keep hitting himself but cannot see the fly buzzing round the leader's head.
- They think it is funny, but they dare not say anything because they know Acti would not want anyone to see

him hit himself and would be angry if he knew they were watching him.
- After this has happened a few times the two young baboons decide that they should do something and go to speak to Hugo, who is a wise older baboon.
- Hugo is also worried and eventually speaks to Acti.
- To Hugo's surprise, Acti gets upset and tells him how the fly is making his life miserable and that even though he is the strongest and bravest baboon he cannot do anything about the fly who is too quick for him to squash.
- Hugo reassures Acti that he is a strong and brave leader but being strong and brave cannot solve all problems. Acti needs to manage the situation.
- Hugo says that the way for Acti to win against the fly is not to hit it but to try to ignore it.
- It is extremely hard for Acti but the next time the fly tries to annoy him he manages to resist trying to squash her and he not only does not hit himself in the face, but he feels better afterwards.
- The fly tries again the following day but again Acti manages to keep his urge to try to squash her under control. The fly gets bored and decides that her fun is over.
- Acti tells Hugo that the fight against the fly has been his toughest ever but his most satisfying.
-

# The Two Best Friends

Mickey and Tommy were best friends. Not because they had been at school together, nor because they played for the same football team. They were friends because they shared a doorway. Mickey and Tommy had both fallen on hard times, they were homeless and spent each night in the doorway of a shop which wasn't being used. They slept in dirty old sleeping bags and all their possessions were piled high in a shopping trolley which had a wobbly wheel. They were often cold and usually hungry, but they had one thing which many people don't have; they had friendship. They had each other, and whenever times were bad, they could talk to each other. If someone kindly gave one of them some food, they would share it and if someone gave one of them some money, they would share that too. They sometimes dreamed of having a warm place to stay, with a front door and a light switch, and a proper bathroom with a mirror, where they could have a bath whenever they wanted and then get dry on big fluffy towels. When they thought about it, they laughed and hugged each other.

They would sometimes go for a walk around the town centre. One day Mickey was walking along by himself, thinking of how much he used to enjoy going out for breakfast. He smiled to himself as he approached 'Pearso's Café' which used to be his favourite. As he walked past, he looked in and saw a poster advertising their new Mega Breakfast. The picture on the poster made his empty tummy do a strange dance. Mickey imagined the massive full English breakfast on the poster was on a real plate in front of him, with four sausages, two eggs, piles of mushrooms, a hill of beans, a stack of fried potato and an enormous tomato, grilled until it had gone black round the edges. He smiled and went off into a little world of his own, thinking about how amazing that meal would be.

Later that day, Mickey was back in the doorway and the two friends were lying on their pile of stuff. Tommy was reading a book which someone had dropped into their trolley. Mickey, however, just could not stop thinking about the Mega Breakfast. It was something he missed so much from his life before things had gone wrong. The day was breezy, and litter and leaves were tumbling down the fairly empty high street.

Mickey was thinking if he preferred eggs fried or scrambled when he felt something hit and stick to his leg. He thought it was just an old crisp packet or some rubbish at first, but when he glanced down, he saw that it wasn't litter. To his shock, it was a twenty-pound note. He couldn't believe his eyes. He reached down and quickly peeled it from his leg.

Then Mickey realised that Tommy had not seen the twenty-pound note. He suddenly had a thought which made him feel strange and uncomfortable. What if he didn't mention the twenty-pound note to Tommy? What if he just put it in his pocket? After all, it had hit *his* leg. It was *his* twenty pounds. He *could* have it. He thought of the Mega Breakfast and persuaded himself that he could keep the money and not share it with his best and only mate. Deep down he knew he should share; he knew he was wrong. He felt guilty for not sharing, but he could almost smell that big breakfast. The sausages, the eggs, the mushrooms, everything.

The next day Mickey said to Tommy that he was going to visit a friend who he hadn't seen for a long time. It was a lie, and he felt bad about telling his friend something which wasn't true, but he just tried not to think about it. Tommy thought it was strange, but if his friend was telling him something, then that was fine by him. He believed him.

Just before eleven o'clock, Mickey left the doorway and headed across town, leaving Tommy reading his book. Mickey by now was excited about the Mega Breakfast he was going to enjoy. He could see it in his mind and could just about taste it, even before he was in the street which had Pearso's Café at the end.

He managed not to think about Tommy, his friend who would be hungry. Mickey entered the café, he sat and asked for the Mega English Breakfast and a mega mug of tea. He then sat waiting, like a child on their birthday before being allowed to open their presents.

When it eventually arrived, the plate was massive, but the food still reached every edge. The beans had to be piled on to the potatoes and the sausages were covered in mushrooms. It was even better than the picture in the window. The tomato was big and black round the edges, just like on the poster and just like Mickey loved them. The tea was hot, and everything was perfect, as long as he didn't think about Tommy, his best friend.

Now strangely, Tommy knew what Mickey was doing, because as Mickey was shovelling the delicious breakfast into his hungry mouth, Tommy was at the window of the café watching. He had decided to go to the library, having finished his book; he wanted to read the next one in the series. As he strolled to the library, he saw Mickey tucking into his massive, tasty breakfast. He didn't understand, and he was a bit jealous but thought there must be a reason that his friend hadn't asked him to go to have breakfast with him. He decided that he wouldn't say anything about it and moved on to get his book.

By the time Mickey had finished his enormous meal, he was as full as he could ever remember. It had tasted great, and his plate was now nearly as clean as it had been when first bought. However, Mickey now felt sick, partly because he had eaten way too much, but also because now the meal was gone all he could think about was his friend, who would have a bellyache for a different reason. Mickey felt very guilty, he had had his meal but now he felt dreadful. He left Pearso's and slowly walked back to the doorway, their doorway.

He decided that he would tell his friend the whole story and he would give him the change from the twenty-pound note, which was three pounds and fifty-one pence. By the time Mickey had got back to the doorway, Tommy was lying there enjoying his new book. As Mickey approached, he felt scared. Was his friend going to be angry? Would Tommy never want to speak to him again? Was he about to lose the best friend he had ever known? He just had to tell Tommy and hope that, in time, things would be ok.

"Oh Tommy, I need to tell you something." He started slowly, and then told Tommy the entire story and ended by telling his friend that he felt terrible, and he was really, really very sorry. He held out the three pounds fifty-one and said he wanted to give him the money so he could buy something to eat. Mickey then waited, terrified that Tommy was going to say that he was furious and didn't want to be his friend anymore.

There was silence which seemed to go on and on, but eventually Tommy spoke. He looked sad as he said, "I am cross with you, Mickey. You are my best friend and I have always shared whatever I have with you. I am really upset that you were selfish and didn't think of me." Tommy looked down at the ground and then lifted his head and looked straight at his friend. His eyes sparkled with the tears which were just managing not to roll down his cheek. "I think two of the most important things about genuine friendship are honesty and trust, and you have hurt me." He paused. "But you know, I think there is something just as important in friendship, maybe even more important, and that is," he paused, "that is being able to forgive. I had the right to expect you to share, but you have the right to expect forgiveness from me because we all make mistakes, and I can see you are truly sorry." He smiled at his friend and put his arm around Mickey's shoulder. "Now let's take our three pounds fifty-one and go buy a couple of cups of tea."

# **THE TWO BEST FRIENDS**

The story of two friends who have fallen on hard times. When one friend lets the other down, they look at their relationship and explore what being a real friend means.

The themes are:

- The responsibilities we have to our friends.
- Relationships are two-way things.
- Forgiveness is an important part of friendship.

**Story map**

- Mickey and Tommy are homeless and are best friends.
- They share everything: food, money, and companionship.
- They are always hungry and often cold.
- Micky sees an ad in a café window for a wonderful full English breakfast.
- He cannot get the picture of the big breakfast out of his head.
- One day when they are both lying in 'their' doorway a twenty-pound note blows onto Mickey's leg.
- He would usually share but he immediately thinks about the breakfast and decides to keep the money for himself.
- He goes on his own to the café and has the enormous breakfast and a huge mug of tea.
- Tommy sees him in the café as he is going to the library but says nothing.

- As soon as Mickey finishes the massive meal, he feels very guilty and decides he must tell Tommy and suffer the consequences.
- When he returns to the doorway, he tells his friend what he has done and waits to find out what Tommy will do.
- Tommy is upset and feels cross with Mickey, but he says that just as he had the right to expect Mickey to share the money, Mickey has the right for his best friend to show him forgiveness.

# The Unhappy Birds

"Pukaw, pukaw," she said, "pukaw, pukaw." She looked sad and forlorn. She stared into space, wearing as near to a frown as a chicken can. She stood still and sad for a long time. Nothing seemed good, everything she could think of was bad. "Pukaw," she said again.

After a while a peacock walked by. The peacock looked even more unhappy than the chicken. "You look miserable," said the miserable peacock.

"I look miserable. Have you looked in a mirror? You look like you've just been told that the turkey has run off and you are next in line for Christmas dinner," the chicken replied, momentarily thinking she was quite funny and then remembering she was miserable and unhappy.

"Well, I am pretty fed up, but tell me what's wrong with you?" The peacock hoped that hearing how unhappy the chicken was might cheer him up.

The chicken looked at the peacock and decided to tell him the problem. "Well, look at me. I am definitely a bird, aren't I?"

"Of course, you're a bird," the peacock said, somewhat puzzled. Where was this going, he wondered? "Carry on," he said, intrigued.

"I know I am a bird, I have feathers and a beak, and I have wings, but that's the problem. Look at my wings." She lifted her short, stubby wings.

"I mean, look at them, they are pathetic. Have you seen me fly? No, you haven't, and shall I tell you why you haven't, because I can't fly, well not more than about 3 metres at a time. Do you know the albatross can fly 10,000 kilometres in a single flight, tiny swifts fly to the other side of the world to keep warm but me, a stupid chicken, struggles to fly the distance a camel can spit. It's just not fair, I tell you, I am fed up with being a chicken. I am worthless. What's the point of being a bird who can't fly?"

The peacock looked even more miserable, and then with genuine honesty said, "Well, you have made me feel even worse because I can't fly much better than you. I'm a useless bird from that respect, but that wasn't what was making me miserable. Well, not until I heard your tale of woe."

"Well, what was making you so glum then?" the chicken asked, hoping to find out she wasn't as badly off as the peacock.

"Well," the peacock started, "I am a bird and every evening and morning I hear the beautiful songs of the song thrushes, nightingales and skylarks. They sing so wonderfully. Everyone likes the dawn chorus or the singing of birds at twilight. Birds provide the world with its music. Well, some birds do, but not peacocks. My voice is awful, just awful, if I try to sing, or even chirp, I sound like one of the humans' car horns." With that, he sat down with a bump and looked very miserable.

Now it was the chicken's turn to feel even more glum. She had felt bad about not being able to fly but she now thought her clucking was hardly comparable with the lovely song of the skylark. So rather than feeling any better, she felt worse.

The two unhappy birds sat in silence, feeling very sorry for themselves. Then, along came a penguin. The penguin was also in a terrible mood. He stopped when he saw the chicken and the peacock sitting quietly, looking fed up. "You two look very miserable," he said.

"Well, you are not exactly looking like it's your birthday either," said the peacock.

"It's OK for you, you don't know how hard it is being a penguin," said the penguin.

"I'm sure it's a lot better than being a chicken," the chicken moaned.

"Or a peacock!" the peacock added. "What's so bad about being a penguin?"

"Well, for a start, look at me," the penguin said, "I look nothing like a bird. My feathers have gone, not like the beautiful plumage of so many birds, my voice is like an alarm and not only can I not fly, I can hardly walk, I just waddle. I am a useless bird, probably the most useless bird there is." With that, the penguin looked down at his feet and sulked. The other two birds said nothing but thought that the penguin did have reason to be miserable.

The three grumpy birds sat there doing nothing, just wallowing in their own misery. They might be there still if the eagle hadn't turned up. Now, the eagle was obviously a strong and scary bird with huge talons on her feet and a hooked beak which could easily have sliced up any of the other birds. When she arrived the other three were understandably nervous.

"You three look like you are trying to decide which one is going to be first for my lunch," the eagle said, laughing. "Don't worry, I am not hungry, you are all quite safe."

"We are not afraid of you," said the chicken.

"Well, we are," said the peacock, for fear of annoying the eagle.

"Well, yes we are," said the chicken, "but that's not the reason we look like this."

"What on earth is the matter then?" the eagle asked.

"We have been thinking about being birds and we have decided that we are not very good birds at all," explained the penguin.

"In fact, we are useless birds," the peacock added.

"We are pathetic, completely pathetic and totally worthless," the chicken felt that she should also say something.

"What do you mean useless and worthless? How come you think that?" the eagle demanded to know.

The three grumpy birds explained to the eagle how they were no good at flying, or singing, or even walking in the penguin's case. They wondered if the eagle would feel sorry for them. Rather than feeling sorry, the eagle lifted her majestic head and laughed. She laughed so loudly that the miserable birds were worried that others would come to see what was happening. They also thought the eagle was being very rude, to find their misery so funny, but they didn't say that because no matter what the eagle said about not eating them, there was no sense in making her angry.

At last, the eagle stopped laughing and spoke. "Well, I don't think you are useless or worthless birds, but I do think you are all fairly silly."

This upset the peacock. "Well, that's very rude of you. What makes you think we are silly?" The peacock suddenly remembered who he was speaking to. "If you don't mind telling us... er... please?"

The eagle realised that the peacock was scared and thought it was hilarious. "Oh, I'll tell you alright, if you will listen. The reason I think you are silly is that you seem to think all birds must be the same, that they should all be able to fly as far as an albatross or as fast as a falcon and that they should all be able to sing as sweetly as a canary, but that's just silly. Chicken, do you know what you are? You are a rubbish flyer, absolutely hopeless and when you sing it sounds like the water draining from a bathtub but that's not what chickens are about, is it? You call yourself worthless, but human beings think of chickens as the most valuable birds in the world."

"Really?" said the chicken, who hadn't really had much to do with humans.

"Yes, really. If it wasn't for chickens, humans would have a completely different diet. They eat millions of chickens every year."

"Well, that's not that good, is it?" the chicken butted in.

"No, I guess not, but even lots of the humans who don't eat chickens love your eggs. You are so important to the everyday life of millions and millions of humans. If most birds vanished humans would hardly notice, but if chickens disappeared, they would not know what to do. You may have limitations in flying and singing, but you are so important, and as for being worthless, you are worth billions."

Well, the chicken felt much better after hearing how very important chickens were. Even if she wasn't too keen on being important as food. She fluffed up her feathers and strutted around feeling quite proud, no, actually very proud.

The peacock was more miserable than ever now.

"Bully for you," he said to the chicken rather ungraciously.

"Oh peacock!" the eagle shouted, "stop being such a dimwit. You are not as important to humans as the chicken is, but just look at yourself."

"What do you mean?" the peacock asked.

"Well, you're not a great flyer either and your voice is like the noise a cat makes when it is stood on by a horse, but look at that tail. Go on, lift it up, go on," the eagle commanded.

The peacock lifted his wonderful tail.

"There, you see, it's one of the greatest sights in the natural world. The peacock has been known for centuries as a thing of great beauty. How can you feel bad about being a peacock with a tail like that? Does an albatross have such a beautiful tail? Does a canary appear on so many beautiful pictures? Of course not."

The peacock looked round. "Do you know," he said, "I had completely forgotten about the old tail. It is rather splendid, isn't it?"

"Of course, it's splendid. You should be proud of such a wonderful gift."

The peacock marched around, flicking his tail, and holding his head high. He was now a very happy peacock.

The penguin looked glum as the other two birds strutted about. The eagle continued. "Penguin, don't look sad. You are unlike any other bird."

"I know," said the sad penguin. "I'm useless!"

"But you are a design triumph," the eagle said, "you may not be able to fly in the air, but you can fly in the sea. You are a genius at living in a place where no other birds can survive. You can swim faster than some fish and your shape is engineering perfection. The best human scientists and designers in the world have struggled to create anything nearly as streamlined and fast. In many ways you are the most advanced bird there is."

"Am I?" penguin asked disbelievingly.

"Yes, you are. Whilst we are all trying to get along here on the ground and in the air, you have evolved into something completely different, and for where you live, different and better!"

"Wow!" said penguin. "That's fantastic... Engineering perfection, me eh... Brilliant!"

And now penguin was strutting (as well as a penguin can strut) with the other two birds.

"You see," said the eagle, "it's all about thinking of the positives. We can all get sad and miserable if we concentrate on the things which aren't as good as we'd like. It's great being an eagle, being strong and powerful and so, so beautiful." She pushed out her powerful chest and held her magnificent head high. "But it's not all fun. No one wants to be your friend because they are all scared of you, and idiot hunters try to shoot you for trophies. You just have to be pleased with what you have."

"You are so wise and clever, eagle," said the chicken, "thank you, you have really helped us all. If there is anything we can ever do for you, please ask."

The eagle gave all three a rather different look. "Well..." she said. "Giving all this advice has made me rather... hungry!"

# **THE UNHAPPY BIRDS**

Three miserable birds are all very down about their failings, each being unhappy about the qualities they don't have. After a real moan, they are helped to see their good points by a passing eagle.

The themes are:

- We should look for positives rather than concentrating on negatives.
- We sometimes need help to see our good points.
- Individuals have different good points even when they share weaknesses.

## **Story map**

- ➢ The chicken is sitting looking very miserable.
- ➢ The peacock arrives also looking miserable.
- ➢ The two birds talk about how miserable they each are.
- ➢ Both birds are feeling very bad about themselves because they cannot sing beautifully like some birds, and they cannot fly very far either.
- ➢ The penguin arrives also looking sad and asks the peacock and the chicken what is wrong with them.
- ➢ When told the penguin is even more sad because both of those deficiencies apply to him but also, he struggles to walk well.
- ➢ A large eagle arrives and asks what is making the birds so glum.
- ➢ When told the problems the eagle laughs and tells the birds that they are silly.

- The birds are angry, but respectfully as they are scared of the big powerful bird.
- The eagle explains that each bird has amazing characteristics which make them special.
- The peacock is an object of beauty and decorates many pieces of art and furniture.
- The chicken is at the centre of a huge industry and the most important bird in the world.
- The penguin is a design miracle and can live in a world in which no other bird can survive.
- The eagle tells them that they all have their own special features and skills and all should be proud of themselves rather than comparing themselves with birds which are completely different.
- The bird says that listening to them has made her… hungry

# The Useless Grasshopper

It was time for the female grasshopper to lay her eggs. She found a soft piece of ground at the edge of a field and pushed her body down into the damp earth. She squeezed out twenty shiny, soft eggs. Then, like grasshopper mums do, she hopped off, leaving her eggs to fend for themselves. The eggs lay there all winter while the snow came and went, and eventually the green shoots of spring started to push through.

Then, one sunny morning, disaster happened. The farmer ploughed the field, and as he turned the tractor, the plough sliced through the clutch of eggs, destroying all of them except one. The single remaining egg eventually hatched, and the little grasshopper nymph crawled into the spring sunlight. She was alone in the world, an enormous world about which she knew nothing.

Grasshoppers, like many insects, are not like little grasshoppers when they are born. They change from a nymph to the adult. The nymphs are little soft-bodied, crawling creatures. Of course, the little nymph didn't know this. In fact, the nymph didn't have a clue what sort of animal she was at all.

It was very difficult for her not knowing what kind of animal she was. She really felt that she needed to find out. She asked a long squidgy-looking creature if he knew, but he said, "Well, you're not a worm, I can tell you that, but I don't know what you are."

She then asked a creature which looked a bit like her. It had lots of legs but a hard shell. "Er... excuse me. Could you tell me what sort of animal you are, please?" she asked nervously.

"Me? I'm a woodlouse," the creature said proudly.

"And what about me?" asked the nymph, "What sort of animal am I?"

"I have absolutely no idea. You certainly are not a woodlouse, but I don't know what you are."

The little nymph carried on her journey asking every animal she met, but none seemed to know. She nearly had a disaster when she asked a sparrow what she thought. The sparrow said that she knew exactly what the nymph was, but then said, "Dinner!"

The nymph just managed to scurry away before the sparrow could peck her up.

Eventually, an old beetle ambled by. "Excuse me," said the desperate nymph, "do you have any idea what sort of animal I am? Please."

The beetle looked the nymph up and down and thought a while and then said, "I think when you grow up you will be a grasshopper. Yes, I'm sure that's right, you are a grasshopper. Now I must dash." And with that, the beetle scuttled away into the grass.

"Aw brilliant!" said the grasshopper, "I'm a grasshopper. I'm a grasshopper, fantastic, that's great." She then thought for a minute and realised that she had no idea what a grasshopper was like or what they did. She was excited but also scared. What if a grasshopper was a horrible animal which was vicious? Or what if they stole things like magpies? Or what if they were the sort of animal that was hated by all other animals like wasps or earwigs? She decided that she had to find out and so she went out to find someone who could tell her what grasshoppers were like.

She now had the same problem as before, only this time she knew what she was, but didn't know what grasshoppers were like. Once again, she asked other animals, this time avoiding birds. At first, other animals either did not know what grasshoppers were like or were too busy to talk to her.

After what seemed like hours, she saw a spider who was dangling from a thread under its web.

"Hello, could you please tell me what grasshoppers are like? And what they do? Please."

The spider, who had met many grasshoppers but didn't realise that the little creature in front of him was a grasshopper nymph, said, "Oh yes, grasshoppers are great, they can jump so far, they have powerful legs. I am quite jealous of grasshoppers."

"Oh, thank you very much," said the grasshopper. She was confused, because she had never felt that she wanted to jump and didn't know how, and her legs certainly didn't feel powerful.

Once the spider had disappeared back up to the web, the grasshopper thought she would see how high she could jump. The answer was very disappointing. She couldn't jump at all. She tried and tried and tried, but nothing. Not even a little hop. Eventually, she slumped down, exhausted, and very, very disappointed. She thought she must be a rubbish grasshopper, if grasshoppers were fantastic jumpers and she couldn't even get off the ground. She wondered if she was the worst grasshopper that had ever lived. She fell asleep thinking what an absolutely useless grasshopper she was.

When she woke up, she was still sad and feeling awful. She now thought she was definitely the worst grasshopper in the world. The grasshopper that couldn't jump, what a pathetic creature. She crawled into the grass and stayed there for a long time. She did nothing much but ate a little and every now and again her skin fell off which was a bit scary at first, but didn't really seem to do any harm. She didn't really care; she just thought she was useless.

One day, a while later, a group of very hungry-looking bugs came running towards her. "Excuse us," they said, "can you help us? We need your help." They seemed desperate.

"My help? Why would anything need my help? I'm pathetic," the sad grasshopper said.

"You can definitely help," one bug pleaded. "You can save our lives!"

"Haha! Save your lives. I doubt that very much."

"Oh, you can. Please help us," another bug said, almost begging.

"Well, if you want me to jump, you are going to be disappointed. I know grasshoppers are supposed to be brilliant jumpers. Well, I am a rubbish grasshopper and I can't jump at all."

The bugs looked very unhappy. "Are you sure?" one asked.

"You look like you could jump a long way," said another.

"Yes, with those big back legs!" a third bug pointed out.

"What big legs?" asked the grasshopper, confused.

"Those legs," the three bugs said, pointing at the legs which the grasshopper had been too miserable to notice growing each time her skin had fallen off.

"Oh," said the grasshopper, who was confused, "where did they come from?"

"I don't know," said a bug, "but if you could just hop up to that ledge and knock those berries down, we can eat and that will stop us from starving."

The grasshopper had been so busy feeling sorry for herself that she hadn't noticed her legs growing. She really didn't know what to think. "Please give it a go," pleaded the biggest bug.

"You don't know what you can do until you try."

"But I tried, and I couldn't jump at all."

"But you have changed, come on, just try."

"Ok. I will. I'll give it a go," the grasshopper said, suddenly feeling brave and quite excited. She mustered all her strength and said to herself, "I have changed, I can do this." And with that thought in her head, she pushed her legs down and leapt way up into the air, actually going straight past the berries on the ledge. She landed back down with a bit of a thump but was OK. In fact, she was feeling very good. The bugs gave a cheer. "Gosh!" shouted the grasshopper. "I can jump and jump really high. I'm not a useless grasshopper at all!" She quickly hopped up and got the berries for the bugs.

"Oh, thank you," they all said at once.

"Oh no," said the grasshopper, "thank you, because you have helped me to realise that I was just not ready to jump before but now I am. Now, I am a brilliant grasshopper." And with that she leapt down the path feeling very, very happy.

# THE USELESS GRASSHOPPER

The story of a grasshopper egg, which hatches not knowing what sort of animal it is. She finds out what she is, but it is a tremendous disappointment because she cannot jump. She does not realise that over time things can change.

The themes are:

- It is important to know who you are.
- You should not give up on yourself.
- You do not know when you will reach your full potential.
- You don't know what you can do until you try.

### Story map

- ➢ A batch of grasshopper eggs is run over by a plough killing all but one egg.
- ➢ The hatched egg is a grasshopper nymph but does not know what she is.
- ➢ She asks lots of the creatures she meets and nearly gets eaten but eventually a beetle says that he thinks she is a grasshopper.
- ➢ She then asks creatures what grasshoppers are like and what they do.
- ➢ Eventually, a spider explains that grasshoppers are great and the best thing about them is that they are great jumpers.
- ➢ The little grasshopper is glad to know what grasshoppers do but feels very bad because she cannot jump at all. She feels that she must be the worst grasshopper in the world.

- She crawls into the grass feeling awful.
- As time goes by, she feels miserable, feeling that she is a rubbish grasshopper.
- One day as the grasshopper is lying in the grass, a group of little bugs who are hungry ask her to jump up and get some berries from a ledge.
- At first, the grasshopper says she cannot because she is a useless grasshopper and cannot jump.
- The bugs beg her to use her powerful legs to jump up and get the berries.
- The grasshopper has not noticed that her legs have been growing over time.
- She gives it a go and finds herself leaping high into the air and reaching the berries.
- The grasshopper realises she is not useless after all and that you don't really know what you can do until you give it a go.

# The Prince, his Friend and the Very Precious Vase

Prince Ashkan was a lucky boy; he was a prince. His mum was the Queen, and his dad was the King. He lived in the enormous palace in the middle of the capital city. Well, he did when he wasn't living in one of the other vast houses or castles which his family owned.

He had all the latest toys as he grew up; he had fantastic sports facilities, and he had incredible holidays all around the world. You would imagine he would be a happy little chap, but he wasn't. Prince Ashkan was lonely.

Ashkan was an only child, he had no brothers or sisters. He had tutors, so he didn't go to school, and he had servants whose job it was to play games with him. They were nice people, but they were grown-ups, and they were all a bit scared of upsetting him.

It seemed like Prince Ashkan had everything any little boy could want, but one thing was missing: A friend. One day he went to see his mum, the Queen.

"Yes?" she said, as he entered the huge hall where the Queen was sitting talking to one of her ministers. "What is it, Ashkan? I am rather busy."

"Well, Mother," he started, "there is something I want."

"Ha, really, something else. Surely you have everything you could want. What is it this time?" The Queen sounded a little angry. She didn't want Ashkan to be spoiled, but she also knew his life was not as easy as people thought. She spoke again, trying to be less harsh. "What is it Ashkan? How can I help?"

"I want to go to school… please," he gulped. He expected his mother to quickly say no, but she said nothing for a while, she was obviously thinking, and then she spoke.

"I see. I'll talk about this with your father, tonight. Now run along, the minister and I have important things to talk about." This shocked Prince Ashkan. He really thought he had no chance.

He was even more shocked the next morning when the King and Queen sat him down and told him that after a long chat, they had decided that it was a good idea that he should go to the school near the palace, because it would give him an understanding of the people and that would be a good thing. He might also enjoy it, they said. Ashkan was stunned, happy and nervous all at the same time, but mostly he was excited at the chance to make friends.

Even though he was a prince he was scared on his first day. The teachers were scared too, and the children were excited. At the end of the first day Ashkan was disappointed; he hadn't found a friend, nor at the end of the second or third. On the fourth day however, he met Peter. They just got on with each other. They ate their lunch together, and they chatted at playtime. Ashkan was happy. He had never had a friend, and now he seemed to have one.

The two boys became close friends and often went round to each other's houses. Peter's mum was very nervous when Ashkan first went for tea, but it was all great. They helped each other; they played football and computer games just like friends do.

As the two boys grew older, they stayed friends and became even closer. They often stayed over at each other's houses, and all the guards at the palace knew and liked Peter. They played a lot of sport and were really competitive. Each loved beating the other and hated losing just as much.

One day they were playing tennis. It was a hot day, and they had been playing for a long time. Peter had won the last four times they had played, and he loved it. Of course, this meant that Ashkan had lost, and he hated it.

This game was very close, and they were both playing well. For the first time in ages, Ashkan believed he could win the match. The game went on and on. Both friends were hot and sweaty. Suddenly, after playing for hours, Ashkan had a match point. He had played so many times against his friend, but he was nervous as he served. He wanted to win so badly. He served the ball deep into the court, Peter hit it back hard and then Ashkan hit another excellent shot, then Peter, it went on and on. Then, Ashkan drove the ball thinking it was a winner, Peter managed to reach it. Ashkan hit the ball to the other side, but again Peter just got to it, this time the ball was easy for Ashkan to hit. He excitedly smashed the ball away from where his friend was, but in his eagerness to win he didn't hit it well, and it was heading towards the line. Ashkan held his breath as the ball bounced. He was sure it was a winner this time.

"Out!" shouted Peter.

"No!" screamed Ashkan, "No way. That was definitely in."

"Ash, I promise, it was out," Peter explained.

"It was in. I saw it." Ashkan shouted.

"But so did I and I'm sure it was out, and it's my call, so it was out." Peter explained. He hadn't seen his friend this annoyed before.

"Look, I'm telling you I saw it land in, that's the truth. I don't lie." Ashkan was getting so worked up.

"Well, I don't lie either Ash, honestly, it was out.' Peter had started to get a bit upset about this; it was spoiling the game.

"Listen, I'm a prince and I don't cheat, it was in!"

"What? You're a prince! What is that supposed to mean?" In all the many years that they had been friends, Ashkan had never mentioned that he was a prince. He had never said anything about being royal or rich. They had always just been friends. Now Peter was cross. "So, you're saying I'm a cheat and because you are a prince, what you say counts. You actually think you are better than me, is that right?" He was now furious with Ashkan. "Well, I'll tell you what, *your highness*, maybe you should find another prince to play tennis with, someone worthy of being your friend." Peter marched over to his bag at the side of the court, picked up his water bottle and towel and stormed away, leaving Ashkan standing in the middle of the tennis court. Ashkan knew he had been wrong. Even though he really thought the ball was in, he knew that Peter wasn't a cheat, and he also knew it was Peter's call. He felt terrible.

The next morning Ashkan was quiet at breakfast. The King and Queen noticed but didn't think much about it. Everyone is quiet sometimes. The following morning however, they started to worry about their son. The morning after that, they could ignore it no longer.

"What's the matter, Ashkan?" the Queen asked.

"Nothing," he answered, but said no more. Like parents usually do, they knew something was wrong.

Two weeks passed, and the King was desperate to know what was wrong with his son. Ashkan hardly spoke to anyone. He didn't go out, and he shouted at the servants and guards, which was something he had never done. The King sent for Ashkan. When he arrived, he spoke firmly to him.

"Now listen, son. Something is wrong and when something is wrong, you need to fix it, otherwise it will stay wrong. If you are going to be a good king, you need to learn to deal with problems."

Ashkan realised that his father was right, so he told him the whole story. He also told his father he accepted that he was wrong. "Then why haven't you gone and spoken to Peter? Go to see him and say sorry."

"I can't," Ashkan said, "I just cannot face him. Although I know I was wrong, I just cannot face Peter."

The King thought and then said, "Follow me, Ashkan." They marched along the long, quiet corridors of the palace. It was an immense place and the royal pair kept walking until they left the usual royal living area with its thick carpets and oil paintings. They went through a heavy door and were at the top of a cold, stone staircase. As they went down the bare stairs, their footsteps now echoed ahead of them. When they reached the bottom, they were standing in front of a huge wooden door which had two large locks and two large, tough-looking guards in front of it. The King waved them aside. "Do you know this room, Ashkan?" he asked.

"Yes. I remember coming here as a child with Mother. It's the treasure room, where all the jewels and precious things are stored."

"That's right, come in." The King unlocked the door, walked into the room and turned the lights on. There was a dazzling display of gold, silver, diamonds and jewels. There were also racks of jewelled swords and clothes and shelves of beautiful glass vases and drinking goblets. The King walked over to one of the racks of fabulous, colourful, delicate glass vases. He took a vase down and handed it to Ashkan. "What do you think of this?"

"Well, it's beautiful, so delicate. Is it very precious?" He asked.

"This is 400 years old. Skilled craftsmen made it. It would be worth many thousands of pounds if it were sold." With that, he took the vase back.

"Why are you showing me this, Dad?" Ashkan asked.

The King looked at his son and then at the vase. He lifted the vase high and then dropped it, deliberately, onto the floor. It smashed into a thousand pieces. "Dad! Have you gone mad?" Ashkan couldn't believe what he had seen his father do. He bent down, looking at the small fragments of coloured glass which had once been such a beautiful piece of art.

The King put his hand on his son's shoulder. "You ask me if I have gone mad, Son, and I can see why you would think that, but that vase was just a thing. A lovely thing, but still a thing which can be bought and sold. You have smashed something far more valuable. Your friendship with Peter has taken years to make, and you have destroyed it, just like I destroyed the vase. You ask me if I am crazy, but what you have done is much greater madness than smashing a vase. Ashkan you still have a chance to mend your friendship. The vase is gone and can never be mended, but you can make things better between you and Peter. You just need the courage to admit that you were wrong and to say you are sorry. If you can learn this lesson, then it will have certainly been worth the cost of the vase."

Ashkan realised that this was a valuable lesson and went straight to see Peter. The first thing he said when Peter opened the door was "I'm so sorry." Peter looked at Ashkan, who he had missed. He smiled and hugged his friend.

# THE PRINCE, HIS FRIEND AND THE VERY PRECIOUS VASE

Prince Ashkan seems to have everything but is lonely and wants a friend. When he is allowed to go to school rather than have tutors, he hopes he will find a friend. When he does, he is happier but eventually needs to decide if his friendship is worth more than his pride.

The themes are:

- Friends are important.
- You cannot put a value on a good friend.
- Sometimes your pride stops you from making good decisions.

## Story Map

- ➢ Prince Ashkan is a very lucky boy.
- ➢ He has everything except a friend.
- ➢ Ashkan is surprised when his parents agree to him going to the local school rather than having his tutors.
- ➢ At first Ashkan is still lonely but then he meets Peter who becomes his friend.
- ➢ As they get older their friendship grows stronger.
- ➢ They have similar interests, visit each other's homes and are seldom apart.
- ➢ They play lots of sports and are very competitive.
- ➢ One day Ashkan thinks he has won a tennis match, but Peter says the shot was out, and it was his call.

- Ashkan says that he does not cheat, and he is a prince. It is the first time that Ashkan has ever made Peter feel that Ashkan feels better than him.
- Peter angrily storms off and tells Ashkan to find a person who is worthy of his friendship.
- Ashkan realises that he was wrong but cannot bring himself to apologise.
- Ashkan and Peter do not talk and Ashkan is very miserable around the palace.
- The King and Queen are worried, but Ashkan will not speak.
- After days the King demands to know what is wrong.
- Ashkan tells him what happened but says that he cannot bring himself to say sorry.
- The King tells Ashkan to follow him and they go to the royal storeroom where he shows him a beautiful vase, made hundreds of years before by great craftsmen.
- Ashkan is shocked when the King deliberately drops the vase, and it smashes into a thousand pieces.
- Ashkan asks why his father would do such a thing. His father tells him that it is broken and can never be mended. He tells his son that he has broken something even more precious, a great friendship, but he has the chance to mend it and he must take it.
- Ashkan realises that his father has taught him a great lesson.
- Ashkan goes and apologises to Peter, who hugs his friend.

# The Most Generous Person in Town

There was once a place which was very competitive. As well as the usual things like football, chess and athletics, they had lots of other competitions: speed hairdressing, ultimate strawberry eating and who had the longest toenails, to name just three. It wasn't just official competitions either, people would just try to win at everything they did. They wanted to be the fastest, biggest, strongest, richest, cleverest, angriest, loudest. It was without doubt the most competitive place anyone knew.

Because people were so busy competing, they never made time to think about other people or to be caring or kind to one another. Because of this, the town was an unpleasant place. They thought being the best was the only thing that mattered. They only cared about what they had and thought the only use for other people was to give them someone to beat.

The mayor of the town realised that the town had turned into an unpleasant place and wanted to do something about it. At first she could not think of anything which would help make it a better place to live. She thought whatever she did it would become a competition and things would just get even worse.

Then she had an idea. She would, after all, have a competition. A competition to see who was the most generous person in the entire town. She thought it would encourage people to be kind and they would try to be nicer than all other people, and that might make the town a better place.

So, they announced the competition; posters went up around the town, adverts were on the TV and radio and messages were sent on Instagram, Twitter and every other type of social media. Everyone was talking about the competition. Because it was a competition, people were keen to be seen as the most generous.

It sort of worked. People tried to be generous, but competitively. One man gave his very expensive watch to a beggar who would actually rather have had a cup of tea and a sandwich. A woman gave her horse to a man, which was nice of her, but he lived on the 23$^{rd}$ floor of a block of flats. On buses and trains no one would sit down because they were all trying to give their seats to other people.

The mayor saw what was happening and thought "Well, at least they are thinking about being generous, even if it is in a fake way, just to win the competition."

Then, one of the very rich people in the town gave a million pounds to poor people. Everyone thought that was amazing and was bound to win. That was until another very rich person gave two million pounds to the local hospital, and a third very rich person walked around the town giving bundles of ten-pound notes to anyone they saw. The mayor was pleased because poor people had more of the money and the hospital could buy more medicine, but she was still worried. She knew that this was just to do with winning the competition.

Votes on the special television programme would decide the competition winner, and it was to be hosted by Sue and Tom, who were very famous and popular. There were four places for candidates on the TV programme but only the three rich people were entered, because no one else thought that they could give as much.

Then, at the last moment, there was another entrant. Suddenly, another name appeared on the TV screen: Séréna Murray, it said. All around the town people were saying:

"Who is that?"

"Is she very rich?"

"What has she given millions of pounds to?"

Nobody knew.

The TV programme started, and each person came on and said why they were the most generous person in the town and why the people should vote for them.

The first rich person came talked about all that she had done for poor people. She had bought them new clothes and put a park in the town near where lots of poor people lived. The audience in the TV studio clapped and cheered.

The second person came on and told all the good things which the hospital could now do, which it couldn't do before she donated two million pounds. The audience cheered even louder.

The third person came on and told how they wanted to be generous to everyone, not just poor or sick people. He then he got a big bag and gave twenty-pound notes to everyone in the audience. They cheered and screamed; they were so happy.

It was finally time for Séréna Murray. Everyone was excited to know what she had done.

Séréna walked in. She wasn't a businesswoman or a wealthy man who had rich parents; she was a little girl. Just an ordinary little girl. A few people sniggered. She was nervous at first as she started to talk.

"Hello, my name is Séréna. I'm not rich or important, but I saw that there was a spare space and thought, if no one else is going to take it, I would. I want to tell you about what I have done. I visit an old lady who lives down my street. Her family live a long way away and she gets lonely. She enjoys talking to me and I like talking to her. We watch TV. I don't really like the programmes she watches, but it's ok.

I didn't give millions of pounds like the other people did, but I buy a sandwich for the homeless lady who sits near the shop at the end of my street, in the doorway. It takes most of my pocket money, but I don't mind; I sit and talk to her whilst she eats. She is very grateful, but it makes me feel good too, and she is interesting. She used to be a rich person, but a few things went wrong in her life and just now she needs some help.

I don't suppose I'll win, but I just wanted people to know that you can be generous without having lots of money. The three rich people are very kind to give such a lot of money, but they have got so much that they won't really miss a million or two. I only get three pounds pocket money and the sandwich costs most of that. Also, I think giving time is often better than money. If everyone gave a bit of time to help others, that would be great. I think sometimes people who don't have much money think they cannot afford to be generous, but being generous is not just about giving money. You can give time or share something you have lots of with someone who hasn't got much."

She had been talking for quite a while on live television, but because she really believed in what she was saying she had forgotten her nerves. They suddenly came back, and she ended by saying, "Thank you for listening." And then she quickly sat down.

There was a moment's silence and then the studio audience burst into loud applause and cheering. It seemed that hearing these things from a young girl had made them all think. They suddenly realised that anyone could be the lady in the doorway and that anyone could one day need help. They also realised that they could all help a bit.

The cheering died down, but before Sue could speak the lady who had given money to the hospital stepped forwards and spoke. "Sue, if I may speak before we go on. I want to say well done to Séréna. She has made me think about what I have done. She is absolutely right. A couple of million pounds does not make any actual difference to me, but the money she gave for a sandwich for her friend is not only most of her money, but it was given because she wanted to help. I didn't give the money to be generous, I gave it to win this competition and this young person has made me realise what a sad and selfish person I am. I am happy for the money to stay at the hospital, but I shall withdraw from the competition."

There was a gasp from the studio audience, followed by loud applause. The first lady now stepped forward and said very similar things and announced that she too was withdrawing from the competition. Again, there was applause, finally the man, with the now empty bag, said he too did not want to stand against someone who was more genuinely generous than him.

So Séréna won the prize, which was a trophy and £10,000. She gave some to the lady in the doorway to help her get somewhere to stay, while she sorted herself out. She gave some to her mum who never had much, and she bought herself a new tablet.

The mayor asked Séréna to speak to the council, and she did. She made them all feel selfish and made them think about how damaging their competitive ways had been to the town.

The town slowly became more thoughtful and genuinely generous. People who didn't have much money gave their time to others who needed it, doing their gardens, their shopping and sometimes just talking to them. The mayor was much happier with the town now a'nd now they were not constantly competing with one another, so was everyone else.

# THE MOST GENEROUS PERSON IN TOWN

In a town where people are only bothered about what they have, the mayor launches a competition to find the most generous person. The results surprise everyone, but the town becomes a better place.

The themes are:

- Being overly competitive can be a bad thing.
- Being generous must be a thoughtful act.
- You can give more than money.
- You don't have to be rich to make a difference.


## Story map

> - A town is a very competitive place; everyone competes with everyone about everything. This makes it an unfriendly place where people are not very nice to each other.
> - The mayor
> - wants to do something to make it a kinder, more friendly place. She announces a competition to find the kindest person in the town.
> - As ever it becomes very competitive, with people doing all sorts of ridiculous things to try to show they are generous.
> - Soon three very rich people do 'big' gestures.
>   - The first gives a million pounds to poverty charities.

- o The second gives two million pounds to the hospital.
  - o The third just walks around handing money out to anyone they pass in the street.
- ➤ Everyone presumes that one of these three will win the final, which is in the form of a TV show with the public voting.
- ➤ Each of the three speaks to the studio audience, who clap and cheer.
- ➤ At the last minute a young girl, Serena, appears and tells the audience the simply, genuinely kind things she has done.
- ➤ Serena says that although the rich people have given lots of money and that was very good of them, she thinks that sometimes being generous is not about money, it's about why you are doing something and what you give.
- ➤ The audience in the TV studio clap and cheer the little girl, who has made them all think.
- ➤ Each of the three rich people come forward and tell the TV show hosts that they want to withdraw from the competition.
- ➤ Serena wins and the town changes for the better.

# **Making Alice Better**

Alice was not very cheerful. She was feeling rather glum. There was no obvious reason that she could think of, she was just miserable. Alice was a young squirrel who lived with her mum, dad and two brothers in a nest in a tree. A squirrel's nest is called a drey. The others all seemed happy. Her brothers were very content if they could wrestle each other and had some hazelnuts to eat, but Alice just couldn't understand why she felt the way she did.

Things carried on like this for a little while and one day whilst she was visiting her lovely grandmother, she told the old squirrel about feeling miserable. "Well," said Gran, who loved Alice very much, "if something is wrong, you need to change something." Alice had heard her say that before and she thought it seemed very sensible. If something was wrong, she should change something, but change what? She couldn't really say why she was miserable, so how did she know what to change?

That night she lay awake whilst the rest of the family were asleep. What could she change? How was she going to alter things, so she felt better? She lay for a long time and then suddenly had a thought. She had always been a good girl. She was polite and did jobs for her family. Other squirrels and animals of the forest always commented about how lovely she was, and her mum and dad were really proud. "Well," she thought, "maybe I should change that". She knew lots of squirrels who were not as well behaved as her. They argued with their parents, didn't help around their drey, and they seemed fairly happy. That's what she would change. She would change the way she behaved, and then she would be happy. She felt a bit scared at the thought of being naughty, but at least she knew what she was going to change.

The next day she woke up early as usual and went out of the drey to go and get breakfast for her family, like she always did. Then she remembered: she wasn't nice, kind, helpful Alice anymore. She was now rude and 'don't care' Alice. She felt bad about not going to get breakfast, but she thought, I have to change something, and this is it. This will make me happy, and she went back to bed without getting breakfast.

As the rest of her family woke up, things started to happen. First her mum came in looking worried. "Are you OK darling?" she asked Alice.

"Yes, I'm fine tha…" But then she stopped herself saying" thank you for asking" as she normally would have. "I'm OK," Alice said, trying to sound tough.

"I thought you might be ill, because you haven't been out and collected the acorns for breakfast. Why not, darling? Is something wrong?"

"No… er, well er… I couldn't be bothered," said Alice. She felt very uncomfortable speaking to her mum like this, but she was changing, and this needed to be done.

"Oh, OK, well I'll go get them then, never mind," said her puzzled and rather worried mother.

Alice said nothing. She didn't feel better; she felt worse.

Breakfast was odd. Alice's brothers were their usual silly selves, but Mum, Dad and Alice were quiet. Afterwards, Dad said, "Do you want to come and help me look for some new oak trees? I think the acorns are running out on the ones round here." Alice liked to go off looking for new trees with her dad and was excited at the thought, but then thought, that's what nice Alice would do, and she wasn't nice Alice anymore.

"Nah," she said, "I can't be bothered." And then she got the same feeling that she had when she spoke to her mum earlier.

"Oh," said a surprised and disappointed sounding dad. "You usually like doing that, but OK I'll see if the boys want to come."

Now it was even worse. Alice felt bad about being rude to her dad, and jealous that her brothers got to hunt for oak trees. This was not working at all. For the rest of the day Alice felt more miserable than ever and eventually decided that being rude and naughty to her parents was not the 'something' she needed to change.

That night, once again, she lay awake thinking what a disaster the day had been and wondering what she could change tomorrow so she would feel better. She thought it should be something good, something which would make people think "gosh" "well done", or "wow, that is very impressive", but what? That was the question. She thought and thought and thought, and then she got it. She knew the 'something' she would change. With a smile on her face, she curled up and went to sleep.

As she woke, she had an excited and quite sick feeling in her tummy. Better than yesterday, but she still felt very tingly and scared. She got up and went to get the things for her family's breakfast. Things were better, back to normal. The brothers were still pains but Alice chatted with her mum and dad like always, apart from yesterday, which no one mentioned.

"What are you going to do today, darling?" Alice's mum asked her.

"Oh, I'm going to go into the Dark Wood." Alice said, trying not to sound frightened. The rest of the family went silent, even the brothers.

"The Dark Wood?!" said Seb, her oldest brother.

"Yes," Alice answered, "the Dark Wood. I have always wanted to see what it's like in there."

"Well, I'm not sure about that, darling," said her dad.

"No, it's a dangerous place with lots of foxes and even some wolves by what people say," said Mum, sounding nervous.

"Well, it's fine. I'm not scared," said Alice, trying to stop her voice from trembling, "because I am…" she paused, "I am brave."

Her brothers laughed. Seb said, "No, you're not! You get scared going up to the top branches of the tree. And you're a squirrel!" They laughed some more, louder than before.

"Well, yes, I used to get scared going up to the top of the tree, but I have changed. I have changed." She said again, trying to convince herself. "I am a brave squirrel, and I am going into the Dark Wood."

"I don't think so, darling," said Dad.

"Well, if she wants to go, then I think she should," said Mum. Dad looked alarmed at Mum, who winked at him so that the children didn't see. Alice wished her mum had forbidden it but then thought if the thing she needed to change to be happy was being brave, then she would do it.

Soon, she was ready to set off for the Dark Wood. She walked slowly along the lane into the heart of the forest. Quickly, it grew dark as the thickly leaved trees got closer together, letting less and less light in. The shadows of the leaves danced around on the floor of the forest. It looked like there were snakes and other creatures all around her, but it was just shadows, she kept telling herself. The wind, which was not strong, seemed to whisper threats which she couldn't quite make out. She grew more frightened but kept going.

She went deeper into the forest and before long she was standing at the entrance to the Dark Wood. She kept telling herself that she was brave, and she wasn't scared; but she was scared. She was terrified. Still, she carried on. She had to change something and now she was 'Brave Alice'. As she moved inside the Dark Wood, the sound was different. The trees were so closely packed that hardly any wind blew through. The rustle of the leaves became a creepy humming noise and just now and again there was the howling of a fox, or was it a wolf? The little squirrel moved deeper into the forest, keeping close to the trees, not knowing where she was going. It was quiet, but each noise sounded loud, close and dangerous. She could not tell where any of the noises were from nor what had made them. She didn't like being 'Brave Alice'.

"Hello." A silky, sickly, slow voice pulled her round as if it was a rope. "And where would a little squirrel be going in the Dark Wood?" the voice asked. She couldn't see who or what was speaking. "It's very dangerous, you know, for a little squirrel to be in here, alone." Suddenly, a fox, the owner of the voice, appeared. It absolutely terrified Alice. She froze to the spot next to a big horse chestnut tree. She tried to speak but her throat was too dry, and the words just sounded like dust. The fox got nearer and nearer, Alice could see its yellow teeth and she could hear her own heart beating loudly in her little chest. She thought this was it, this was the end. The fox was definitely going to eat her. He came closer and closer… and closer.

Alice closed her eyes. Oh dear, she never found out what she needed to change. She was now sure it wasn't being brave because this was where that had got her. The fox was almost there, she could smell its stinky breath. She knew this was the end, she would never see her family again. She thought of how devastated her parents would be, even her brothers would be sad. This was it, the end of Alice. She took a deep final breath and… suddenly she felt herself lifting off the floor, something from above grabbed her and lifted her high into the big horse chestnut tree, just as the fox jumped at her. The fox didn't grab the little squirrel, he smashed his head into the bottom of the tree. Alice gave a squeal, partly of surprise and partly of terror, as her parents lifted her to safety. As soon as she realised that it was them, she hugged them as if she would never let go.

"You didn't think we would let you go into the Dark Wood on your own, did you?" Mum asked. "We've been following you. Now come on, you can explain all this strange behaviour when we get back to the drey." And off they went through the treetops, out of harm's way until they were back at their tree and in their home. Gran was there too. She had been told of Alice behaving strangely and was worried. They sat there looking at the little squirrel.

"So," said Dad, "what's the matter? One day you behave like you are trying to make us not like you and the next day, you try to become fox food. What has happened?"

Alice was very upset now. She had been rude and then, even worse, had put her parents in danger in the Dark Wood. "Well Gran said that when you feel things aren't right, you need to change something, so I tried. I changed from being good and well-behaved to being rude and naughty, but that didn't work. Then I thought I would change from being a scared squirrel to being brave, but I don't think I am very brave at all. I was really, really scared in the Dark Wood." The little squirrel started to cry, and her Gran hugged her.

"Well," said Dad, "for what it's worth, I think you were very brave, because you were scared and still went in there. You were also rather silly, but you were certainly brave."

Gran spoke. "When I said you need to change something I didn't mean just change anything, changing to be rude wouldn't ever help, and you are brave, you don't need to do silly dangerous things to prove that."

"But what should I change then, Gran?" Alice asked.

"Well," said the old squirrel, "everyone feels down at times. Everyone sometimes feels a bit glum and the first thing we should try to change is how we see ourselves. When you feel low and miserable, things seem bad, but actually they aren't usually as bad as they seem. You have a loving family, a good place to live and two very annoying but lovely brothers, who are great. You are a fantastic squirrel, loved by everyone, helpful, kind and yes, brave. The thing you really need to change is how you see yourself and you need to recognise all the great things about Alice."

# **MAKING ALICE BETTER**

The story of a young squirrel who is feeling low. She wants to change things. She tries to be things she is not and puts herself in danger. The message is to appreciate yourself for the good things about you. The only thing to change sometimes is the way you see yourself.

The themes are:

- Look for the positives in yourself.
- Don't try to be what you are not.
- Sometimes you need to accept who you are.

## **Story map**

- ➢ Alice is a squirrel who is not feeling very happy.
- ➢ She does not know why she is miserable.
- ➢ She recalls what her Gran has always said; that if something is wrong you need to change something. She wonders what she could change.
- ➢ She is a very helpful girl, who is well-behaved and always does the right things, so she wonders if she would feel better if she changed that. She decides to be rude and unhelpful.
- ➢ Her parents worry about it, and she hates it and feels worse.
- ➢ She is a timid girl, so she wonders if she should try to be braver.

- The next day she decides to show that she is brave and goes to the very scary Dark Wood which is full of dangers.
- Her family are very worried about this and try to persuade her not to go there but she insists that she has changed and is now 'Brave Alice'.
- She is frightened as she sets off to the Dark Wood, which is a horrible scary place.
- Once in the wood a fox approaches her, and she is terrified.
- The fox gets closer and closer and just as it jumps at her she is lifted up by her parents.
- When they get home her parents, and Gran, who has come to make sure she is OK, want to know what is going on.
- Alice explains that she felt she should change things because her Gran had said if things are not right you should change them.
- Her parents explain that she needed to talk to people and maybe change how she saw herself.

# The Wisest Princess

The Queen was getting old. She had been a good queen and had made sure that the people of her land were treated fairly and had enough to eat. She was worried that she would soon have to hand over the running of the country to one of her two twin daughters, Pina and Nami.

When the twins were born, the Queen only allowed the royal midwife, who was an old, loyal and faithful woman, to be present. The midwife was sworn to secrecy, so no one other than the Queen and the midwife knew which daughter was born first.

The midwife had long since died, and so now only the Queen knew which of the princesses was the oldest. She had kept it a secret, so she could choose which princess would be best to rule the country after her. Now the time was approaching when she would have to make the big decision.

One morning, the Queen summoned her two daughters to her chamber. "I have a task for each of you," she calmly explained. "You shall each take charge of an island which is off our shore. They are currently uninhabited, and I have found groups of people who all wish to start new lives. Each of you will be in charge of one group and will decide how your own island runs. You must try to be fair and to help the people to be happy and have good lives. Of course, that includes having enough to eat." She walked over to the window and gazed out over her kingdom. "You will each have a ship, goats and chickens, grain and some tools. It is up to you how you give these out and how you use the land of the island. Each has flat plains which will be wonderful for growing crops. Each island also has mountains, forests and beaches. The ships are ready, as are the people. You have a day to prepare, and you will leave tomorrow afternoon."

The princesses were surprised, but they knew their mother was testing them, and they knew why.

The next day came quickly, and the princesses arrived at the port ready for the adventure and challenges which lay ahead of them. They hugged and wished each other luck then walked over to their ships, which had cheering, waving people hanging over the rails, shouting to their families and friends who had come to wish them well in their new lives. The helpful wind quickly took the ships out of port and soon they were over the horizon.

Pina and Nami were nervous; they wanted to be fair but had different ideas about what being fair meant. Pina felt that if people worked hard, they would be OK. They should be responsible for themselves and their families and not rely on other people. Everyone should be able to look after themselves. Nami was different. She thought it was best if people shared their efforts and what they produced so that everyone had an equal chance to contribute. She felt that those who had more should give to those who had less.

Pina's ship landed first. It was a beautiful island. The bay where the ship landed was surrounded by golden beaches which were edged by mountains and forests to the east and west, with long green grasslands to the north. The sky was as blue as the sea, and the sun sat in the sky like the yolk of an egg. The captain of the ship handed Pina a map of the island as the Queen had instructed. Pina decided that she would divide the entire island into plots. She gave each plot of land a number and then someone from each family came and picked a number out of a sack. The number they picked decided which plot of land the family would own.

Each family got one plot of land, along with a goat, three chickens, a sack of grain and some tools. "Go to your land and make a home there. Build a house and plant your grain. You should live off grain, milk from your goats and eggs from your hens. People who work hard will be fine," she told her people.

When Nami's ship landed, she also had a map and a beautiful island, but she had decided to do things differently. She gave each person a smaller plot of land on the edge of the forest, on the foothills of the mountains or by one of the beaches. Unlike Pina, she didn't give any of the people grassland to build on. She said that they would all work on that land together.

And so, the people of each island worked hard and tried to make a good life for themselves. On Pina's Island things were hard, especially for the people who had been given land on the mountains and by the beach. Their seeds did not grow well. On the mountains, the grain just bounced on the rocks and lay waiting for birds to come and eat it, which they did. The seeds did try to grow a little on the beaches but could not reach down to find fresh water. The tiny plants which did grow soon withered and died. The people all worked hard, but the crops did not grow, and there was hunger. Of course, the people who had been lucky enough to be given plots on the grasslands had lots of crops. They worked hard, gathered in their harvest and stored their grain.

On Nami's island, things were different. The people all lived around the island but worked together on the grasslands. They all worked hard and grew lots and lots of food. The people harvested their crops and stored the grain, and each took what they needed. They felt like a team, because they worked together, and they felt the other people on the island were their friends.

Unfortunately, things got worse on Pina's island. The people with no food asked the people who had farms on the grassland to help them by sharing their grain. The grassland farmers said that they had worked hard and the crops they had grown were theirs. The hungry people grew angry and there were very bad feelings between those who had food and those who had none.

Because they had grown more food than they had needed on Nami's island, they were able to trade with merchants and received some money, which they used to build a hospital and a school. People had a say in what happened on the island, but also felt that the Princess had their best interests at heart.

On Pina's island, no one was happy. The hungry people had now become the starving people. They had taken to eating whatever they could find. They had eaten their chickens and goats. They hunted in the forest and even stole from the food stores of the people on the grasslands. The people on the grasslands were not happy either. They lived in fear of the hungry people, they hated them and viewed them as a threat. To them, they were the enemy.

The Queen sent her advisors to the island every few months. They looked around but they said nothing until they got back to the Queen and told her how things were on each of the islands.

After three years, the Queen decided to see for herself. She arrived on Pina's island in the royal galleon. She had not warned her daughter, because she wanted to see how things really were. She looked around and saw that the island was not a happy place. It had people who were sick, angry and hungry. There was little fairness and even less happiness. After she had toured the island, she asked Pina why it was like this. "I don't know," Pina said with a voice which showed that she was as unhappy as the rest of the island. "I asked them to work hard, and I thought they had, but maybe they didn't. Maybe this island just cannot produce enough to feed this number of people."

"Come with me," the Queen held out her hand towards the sad princess. She guided Pina towards the royal galleon, which quickly set sail towards Nami's island.

When they landed Pina was amazed with what she saw. She could see lots of people in the fields, which were full of crops. She could see children filing out of the school and a group of people outside the small hospital. "How has this all happened in just three years?" she asked. "This island must be better than mine. It's not fair that she got such a lovely island."

"The islands are the same," the Queen said, "the difference is that here there is fairness and friendship; on your island there is inequality and anger. Here there is teamwork and community; on your island there is greed and hatred. Can you see how when people work together to get the best out of their place, they can do so much more?"

Pina looked around and sighed. She smiled at her mother and said, "I'm sorry, Mother. It is my fault. I gave people land where they couldn't possibly survive, and then I got angry and accused them of not working hard enough. I thought that if people worked hard, they would be fine, but I was wrong. Clearly Nami is wiser than me, I think that when it is time for you to step down, she should be Queen."

The Queen smiled, "You did what you thought was right, and you have shown that you realise you were wrong. I am sure that you have learned a great deal from this. You made a mistake, which everyone can do. I think you have learned an important lesson, and hopefully you will help your sister when she becomes Queen. She has great wisdom, which is good, but you have the humility to accept when you are wrong and that is also a noble thing."

A year later, the Queen stood down and they crowned Nami as the new Queen with her sister at her side. After the coronation they stood on the palace balcony, and the crowds cheered their new monarch.

One of the old Queen's most trusted servants asked, "Excuse me, Your Majesty. Now that you have stood down, we would all like to know: which one of the princesses was born first?"

The Queen smiled at him and said, "The honest truth is… I can't remember!"

# THE WISEST PRINCESS

The Queen wants to know which of her daughters will make the best queen when she steps down. She gives them a test, and each Princess reacts differently, which shows the Queen who should be the next monarch.

The themes are:

- You need to think about everyone.
- Sometimes people cannot thrive even if they work hard
- People can work together for the greater good.
- It is better for everyone to be OK rather than some rich and some poor.

## Story map

- ➢ The Queen has been a good queen and now wants to know which of her twin daughters should take over from her.
- ➢ She devises a test to find the princess who will be the best queen.
- ➢ Each princess is given a similar, uninhabited island, a ship full of people who want to start a new life and some food, livestock and equipment.
- ➢ The Queen tells them to rule the island the way that they feel best.
- ➢ One princess divides her island into areas and randomly gives each family a plot of land to make into a farm. Some get great places to grow food and build a house, others are less lucky and get places which are not so good.

- The other princess sees that some parts of her island are good for growing food, so she gives smaller plots to people, and they all come together to work as a team, many farm, some fish, some look after children.
- Over time, the people on the first island fare differently. Those lucky ones with good land do well and those with less good land do less well. There is resentment and anger on the island.
- On the second island, there is greater equality. Everyone shares the food which is produced and there is enough. They also have some to sell, which they do, and they build a school and a hospital.
- The Queen takes the princess from the first island to the second island to see how her sister has organised things.
- The first princess realises that her sister had been wiser and should be queen.
- The Queen makes her choice and soon stands down.
- When asked which is the oldest princess, she cannot remember.

# The Crossroads

A man walked down the road to the edge of his town and came to a crossroads. He stopped, scratched his head, rubbed his chin and then started to cry. After a short while, he sat down and continued to sob.

Shortly afterwards, a woman walked along the same road and she too reached the crossroads. She stopped, looked up each of the other roads, then sniffed and also cried. She also then sat down, sobbing.

A few minutes later, a third person came along the road, stopped and collapsed in tears. All three sat there at the crossroads for several hours, sobbing and occasionally wailing.

In time, an old man walked along the road. He looked at the three unhappy travellers. He then carried on, turning left at the crossroads. After a while he stopped, turned round and went back to where the curious group were sitting.

He talked to the first man, who was still very tearful. "Why are you just sitting there, crying?"

"Well," said the wretched man, "I was perfectly happy walking along this road until I arrived at this crossroads, and now I'm stuck here. I don't know which way to go." The man buried his head in his hands and cried.

The old man then spoke to the woman. "Excuse me, what's the matter? Why are you sitting there and sobbing in such a sad and distraught manner?"

"Well, I was walking along this road, I thought I knew where I was going, then suddenly this crossroads is here, and I just don't know which way to go."

Now the man turned to the third traveller and said, "Excuse me, but are you also crying and sitting there because you don't know which way to go?"

"Well, yes," said the man, "that's right. I thought I knew where I was going, but this crossroads has made me doubt myself."

The old man returned to the first distraught gentleman, who was in a crumpled heap, sniffing. He spoke kindly to him. "Why are you so upset? Why don't you know which way to go? Why are you walking along this road?"

The man looked up and said, "I want to get as far away from this town as possible. I have had a big argument with my family, and I need to get away from them all. I love them very much, but I can't cope with them being upset with me. I just need to get away."

Now the old man moved forward towards the woman, who had calmed down a little. She sat staring, with tears in her eyes. "Why are you so upset?" he asked.

"Well, I was so excited about making my way in the world. I wanted to work hard and meet lots of new people. I had real purpose in my life, but now I have doubt about which way to go. I wasn't expecting to have to make such a decision so soon in my journey. I don't know which way to go, I just don't know." She started to weep again. The old man moved on to the final traveller, who was looking very anxious as he sat waiting to answer the questions which he knew were coming.

"What is causing you so much upset, my friend?" he enquired.

"Well, I keep wanting to move away from the town, I need a fresh start in life, but every time I get to this crossroads, I can't decide which way to go. I sit here trying to decide but end up just heading back to the old town, and my old life which has made me so unhappy."

The old man thought for a moment and then wandered back to the first man and spoke to him. "My friend, you are running away from your troubles, but no matter how far away you run the troubles will still be there. You say you love your family, but the further you are away from them the deeper the pain will be. The reason you don't know which way to go is because you don't really want to go. The road you need to take is the one you have come along. The one which leads back to the town where your mother and father are waiting to sort out this family problem. You are leaving this town for the wrong reason. If you want to move forward with your life, then you must go back and deal with your problems, then the path to take will be obvious."

The man looked up with clearer eyes. Slowly, a smile spread across his face. "Of course," he said, "why didn't I realise that?" He stood and grasped the old man by the hand and shook it. "I am going to go to speak with my family straight away and sort this out. I have been such a fool. Thank you, stranger, whoever you are; you are a wise man. Thank you so much!" With that, he ran back down the road towards the town.

The old man smiled and then headed towards the woman who had been watching what was happening. She said to the old man, "I hope that you are not going to tell me to go back to town. I want to go on and move forward with my life. I feel I can make a difference to the world. I just don't know which way to go." As she said this last sentence her shoulders rounded, and her enthusiasm vanished.

"Oh, I don't think you should go back to the town. You are clearly ready to leave this place and I am sure that you will do well. Do you know what lies at the end of these roads?" the old man asked, pointing at each of the roads in turn.

"No, I don't, and that's what makes it so difficult to choose," she replied.

"I disagree," the old man said. "You say you just want to make your way in the world. You know that the world is down each of these roads, so it really does not matter which one you choose. You should just go down any road because you are a positive person, and you will do well as long as you continue to believe in yourself. Whichever direction you take is the right direction."

The woman lifted her head and smiled. "You're right, it doesn't matter which way I choose because I'm going to do well wherever I go. Thank you, thank you very much," and with that she stood, picked up her bag and set off straight ahead. The old man watched as the young woman marched forward. He knew that she would be OK; in fact, he had a strong feeling that she was going to be a great success.

Now he turned to the third traveller, who had been watching what was happening and was scared about what the old man was going to say to him. "Do you think it's obvious what I should do?" he asked the old man.

"Well, yes and no," said the wise elder. "You know what you want to do but lack the courage to do it. You are clearly a worrier. You need someone to tell you it will be OK, but you are the only one who can say this. Your choice of road is not about the route you take, but about how much faith you have in yourself. I cannot tell you, only you can answer this question."

"OK," said the now fairly confused younger man, "ask me."

"Before I ask, I need to know what you believe you will achieve by leaving this town?"

"I have nothing to keep me here. I have no friends and no job. I need a new start. I'm not running from anything; I just need a new start somewhere else."

The old man smiled. "OK, if you wait until next year to leave town, would it be better than today?"

"Not really," said the young man.

"And what if you leave next month? Would that be better than today?"

"I don't think so," said the man.

"How about next week?" the old man asked.

"No, no, better at all," the younger man thought he knew what the old man was getting at.

"What if you left tomorrow?" the old man questioned.

"No better at all."

"In an hour?"

"No, I don't think any time will be better than right now," said the younger man with a new confidence in his voice.

"Well, you have answered your own question. Well done!" said the old man with a knowing grin.

"I have, haven't I?" said the young man. "If I'm going to move on, I just need to get on with it." He picked up his bag and set off.

After he had taken a few steps, he turned to thank the old man, but when he looked back, there was nobody there.

# THE CROSSROADS

Three travellers all reach a crossroads at the edge of town and are all in some distress. A wise old man helps each of them to solve their problems by explaining the actual causes for their anxieties.

The themes are:

- Although problems might seem the same, they can be very different.
- Sometimes you need someone else to help you understand your problems.
- You need to deal with problems, not run from them.

### Story map

- One at a time, three people approach a crossroads, walking away from a town.
- Each one stops at the crossroads, sits down and cries.
- An elderly man walks along the road and goes past the crossroads but then turns and goes back to the people sitting by the road weeping.
- When he asks the first man what the matter is he is told that the man cannot decide which way to go. He cannot make the decision.
- The woman, when asked, also says that she does not know which way to go.
- The third traveller says that seeing the crossroads has made him doubt if he should be leaving town.
- The man returns to the first traveller who says that he needs to get away from the town because he has had a big argument with his family. He does not know which way to go because he just wants to get away from town.

- The woman now tells the old man that she was excited about leaving but she wasn't expecting to have to make a decision so soon and she was scared.
- The third traveller says that he has tried to leave the town several times because he needs a fresh start but each time when he arrives at the crossroads he can go no further.
- He returns to the first traveller and says that he is running away from the argument with his family and however far he goes, the problem will still be there. He needs to make peace with his family before he leaves.
- The man realises he is right, stands up and heads back to town, much happier.
- Then he goes to the woman, who says that she needs to leave the town but does not know what is at the end of any of the roads and this makes it hard.
- The man says he disagrees, he says that he is confident that she can do well and so she should just pick a road and get on with it. He says any road is the right road because she believes in herself, and she can do well.
- The woman says he is right and stands and strides down the road at the far side of the crossroads.
- The third traveller says that he has no job, family or friends to keep him in the town but is scared to actually leave and move on with life.
- The old man says that he is stopping himself moving on in life.
- He asks the young man if it will be any different if he delays a year, a month or a week. The answer is no, and the young man realises that he should just get on with it. He walks up the road.
- When he looks back the man is not there.

# The Curious Rabbit

Lionel was a rabbit, and an average-looking rabbit it has to be said. Long ears, like rabbits have. Pretty big teeth, like rabbits have, and reasonably powerful back legs for hopping and jumping, just like rabbits have. Nothing remarkable at all, you might think. However, if you did think that you would be wrong, very wrong, because Lionel was not a run-of-the-mill rabbit, not an everyday bunny, and not at all average.

The thing which made Lionel exceptional was curiosity. Lionel was a very curious rabbit indeed. He wasn't happy to just know that something happened. Oh no, he wanted to know why it happened, or how it happened. It wasn't enough to tell Lionel that something was there because he would want to know where it had come from.

Sometimes, Lionel's mother would get frustrated with him when he asked why, when, and what, because sometimes she had other things to do and other times, she simply did not know the answer.

She didn't know why trees were so tall, or why the sun was yellow, or why the wind is there but you can't see it! As Lionel got older, he became more curious and whenever his mother did not know the answer, he would either try to find out, or at least would spend a great deal of time just thinking about what the answer might be.

One sunny day, Lionel and his mother were in the bottom field nibbling young shoots of grass, when it started to rain. Mother said that they should shelter until the shower had passed, but Lionel was mesmerised by what he could see in the sky. There, arching high over the hills, was the most spectacular rainbow you can possibly imagine.

"Look!" gasped Lionel. He had never seen a rainbow before. Mother knew he would want to know all about rainbows and especially, that he would want to know where they end. She was completely correct.

"Where does it end?" he asked enthusiastically.

"I'm sorry Lionel, I really have no idea. No one knows where rainbows end!"

"Well, someone must know, goodness me!" Lionel said, thinking his mum really should care more about these important things. This was a big moment in Lionel's life, and he became obsessed with finding out where rainbows touch the Earth.

The day after seeing the amazing rainbow, Lionel set off toward where it had seemed to go. Obviously, it wasn't there anymore, but he had really looked hard and remembered the part of the hill where the rainbow had crossed. He walked and walked, further than he had ever walked before.

On his journey, he saw a stream which he had never seen before and he found another family of rabbits, which he did not know about; it turned out that they were his cousins.

He carried on walking in the direction of where he thought the rainbow must have landed, but he could find no sign of it. Eventually, he decided that he needed to return home. When he got back to his burrow, his mum asked if he had found where the rainbow had come from or where it had gone. "No," he said rather sadly, "but I found a stream I didn't know about and a branch of our family that I had never heard of."

"Oh, that's interesting, I don't know of a stream over that way, nor any relatives. You have made a couple of discoveries, Lionel!" said his mum, feeling quite proud.

Lionel just wanted to know more about rainbows. The next time there was a rainbow he set off to find where it touched the Earth straight away, whilst it was still raining and whilst the rainbow was still in the sky. He chased the beautiful arch across the fields. On the way he found a carrot patch which was new and he saw that the humans had built a tunnel under the road, which made it much safer to get to the top fields. He had made two more discoveries, he thought to himself. But no matter how far he ran, he never got to the place where the rainbow met the ground.

Every time there was a rainbow, Lionel would head out to find where it touched the Earth. He nearly always found new things, but never found out where rainbows come from or go to.

One day, he returned from one of his journeys, again having failed to find the rainbow's end. All the other rabbits were waiting and cheered as he arrived back. Lionel was shocked. "Why are you all cheering me? I failed again. I don't know where rainbows come from or where they go to. I am a failure. Why would you cheer me?"

MacGregor, the chief rabbit of the whole burrow, stepped forward. "Well," he said, "you may not have found the place that rainbows go or come from, but when you go on your journeys, you make fantastic discoveries which help every rabbit in the burrow to have better lives, and although you might think you are a failure, we all think you, and your curiosity, are absolutely fantastic."

They all cheered again, and Lionel felt great, and just then it started to rain, and a beautiful rainbow appeared. "Right," said Lionel, "I'd better be off to find where that comes from and is going to. I probably won't find out, but the great thing is that there are so many things in the world which we don't know about. Who knows what I will discover? One thing is certain; if you don't look you will never find out." ... And off he went.

# THE CURIOUS RABBIT

The story of a young rabbit who wants to know where rainbows end and is determined to find out. Although he never solves this problem, his curiosity results in him finding lots of other things which none of the other rabbits knew before.

The themes are:

- It is good to follow your dreams.
- Being curious leads to discoveries.
- We need curious people to make discoveries.
- You don't find things if you don't look

## Story map

- ➢ An apparently normal rabbit is a very curious animal.
- ➢ He asks his mum lots of questions which she tries to answer but sometimes cannot.
- ➢ One day the rabbit sees a rainbow and is transfixed.
- ➢ He wants to know where it goes and where it touches the ground. His mum does not know.
- ➢ Each time there is a rainbow, he sets off to find the answers but never does. However, he does find a whole variety of other useful things, such as another group of rabbits, a tunnel under the motorway and a new carrot patch.
- ➢ The rabbit gets despondent, but the rest of the rabbit warren celebrate that because of the curiosity of the little rabbit they all have better lives.

# The Javelin

Xandro was not keen on sport. He liked nothing about it. He didn't like that everyone judged him on how fast he could run or how well he could catch or shoot. He hated getting changed with all the other children and he hated wearing shorts. Every PE lesson was a chore, and every week he would have an argument with his PE teacher. If it wasn't because he had forgotten his kit or that he said he was unwell, it was because the teachers said that he wasn't trying - he usually wasn't.

Rather strangely, Xandro's best friend Mina was fantastic at sport. She was the captain of the football team and the netball team and was one of those annoying people who seemed to be good at any sport she tried. The PE teachers all loved Mina and smiled whenever she walked into the gymnasium. One day Mina and Xandro were talking.

"But I don't understand why you hate sport so much. You don't really give it a go. You might be better than you think. You might be a natural!" Mina told her friend.

"Oh, yeah!" said Xandro, "I'm naturally rubbish, naturally a joke, naturally an object of fun for you sporty types."

"No, you just will not try. Why not?"

"Because I don't want to mess up and make a fool of myself." Xandro said, with a sigh; they had this conversation at least once a week.

Mina shook her head and smiled at her friend, "You are silly! Come on, it's your favourite time of the week: PE!" she said, teasing Xandro, who screwed his face up and pretended to be sick. "I'm looking forward to it, it's athletics today," Mina continued, smiling.

"It's OK, I've got a letter from my mum saying I have a bad leg and can't do it." He smiled, knowing that he had nothing wrong with his leg. He had persuaded his mum to write the letter by doing lots of chores around the house and babysitting his younger brother. His mum hadn't liked sport when she was at school and didn't mind Xandro missing PE.

Mr Edge, the PE teacher, was a decent bloke, but he hated when people didn't take his subject seriously. He knew that not everyone was gifted at PE, but he thought they should at least try. When Xandro handed over the letter, Mr Edge knew what it was by the slight smile on Xandro's face. "OK Xandro," he said, after reading his mum's note. "It doesn't look too bad to me, but I will not go against your mother. You can help do some measuring and fetch the equipment."

Xandro didn't mind this. It was a nice day and once he had got the equipment out, he could just use the big tape and measure how far the other kids had pointlessly hurled a javelin. As it was javelin, he had to wait away from the place they landed in case he got speared. He always thought it would be funny if a javelin stuck into someone who then staggered to a new world record, and then collapsed. But he didn't want that person to be him, so he kept an eye on the throwers, just in case.

The lesson passed quickly and Xandro actually got quite interested. There was a close competition between Mina and Stevie Hardy, and Mina won with the last throw, so he was happy about that. He didn't really like Stevie, although he realised that this was because he was jealous of him. Stevie was good at sport, popular, and his mum had a flash car. He was actually a friendly lad, but Xandro still thought it was OK to decide he didn't like him. Mr Edge told Xandro to put the javelins away, and to be careful. Then the entire class, including Mr Edge, marched off towards the changing rooms.

When he was on his own, Xandro looked down at the javelins which were lying by the throw line. He suddenly fancied a go. He knew that Edgy would give him triple detention if he found him throwing a javelin with no adult there, but he thought "just one throw". Mina's winning throw was just over 21 metres. He didn't think he could get anywhere near that, but it would be fun to find out.

When he was certain no one else was watching and ready to make fun of him, he picked up a javelin with an orange and green grip running around the middle. He took a few paces back from the throw line, had a last look around, felt a bit naughty, and took four quickening paces towards the line before swinging his arm forward like he had heard Edgy telling the kids to do. He felt the muscles in his legs, bum, back, ribs, shoulders and arm tighten and release like he was some precision machine. It all felt right. As his hand flew forward, it released the long wooden javelin as it was just past his head and the spear took flight like a startled bird, its tail wiggling with the power pushing it ever further. On and on it flew, straight, forward and upward. Then it reached its maximum height and started to head towards the grass, but still quickly moving forward. When it eventually landed, it was a long way from where Xandro stood open-mouthed, half hoping someone had seen his throw because it would be worth a triple detention; he had beaten Mina by a good eight metres!

"Come on, Xandro, get a move on!" Mr Edge shouted, as he stood at the entrance of the changing block. He obviously hadn't seen the throw. "Don't forget that one over there," the

PE teacher said, pointing at Xandro's javelin. There was no way he was going to forget that javelin, ever.

He told Mina, but she just said, "Yeah, of course, and did you jump the length of the long jump pit as well?" then she laughed. He wanted to argue but thought she wouldn't believe him, so he said no more.

He told his mum. She believed him, which he was pleased about. "You see," Xandro's mum said, "you never know how well you can do something until you give it a go!" and she was dead right. From that day on, Xandro gave things a go. Sometimes he did OK, sometimes he did well and sometimes not so well.

No one else really cared that much, but he did and he always 'gave it a go'. And hoped it wouldn't be too long before they did javelin again!

# **THE JAVELIN**

Xandro will do anything to avoid PE and sport in general. He does not want to be teased by others and always has an excuse. When he has a go when no one is looking, he realises that you don't know how good you are until you try.

The themes are:

- You don't know how good you are until you give it a go.
- You shouldn't worry about failing.
- You can surprise yourself if you try.

## Story map

- ➢ Xandro hates sport because he feels that he is no good and he thinks everyone laughs at him when he does not do well.
- ➢ Mina, who is Xandro's best friend, loves all sport and is very good at it. She tries to get Xandro to get involved in PE more but fails.
- ➢ Xandro will do anything to get out of PE lessons and gets his mum to write a note saying he is not fit to do it.
- ➢ Mr Edge, the PE teacher tells Xandro that he can help with the equipment. They are doing the javelin, so he must be careful.
- ➢ Xandro quite likes helping with the lesson and is very interested in who will throw the furthest. Mina and Stevie Hardy are the best and very good.
- ➢ Mina wins with the last throw. Xandro is happy.
- ➢ At the end of the lesson, Mr Edge asks Xandro to carefully put the javelins away.

- The rest of the class disappear into the changing rooms leaving Xandro and the javelins. Suddenly he has an urge to have a go. He knows that he really shouldn't.
- He picks up a javelin and goes to the line from where the children were throwing.
- He remembers what Mr Edge had said and checks he is not being watched by anyone.
- He throws it and the javelin just flies. On and on, further and further, he is amazed as the javelin just keeps going. It even goes further than Stevie's and Mina's. He would have been the best in the class. He almost wishes someone had seen.
- Mina won't believe him, but his mum does, and says it just goes to show that you should give things a go because you don't know how good you are at something until you try.

# A Matter of Pride

Mrs Cresswell told the class her to look at her, like she always did on Friday afternoons. She said, "Nearly the weekend - now for the homework." It said the same on the interactive whiteboard which Mrs Cresswell was leaning against. She did this every week.

The class, who had been putting their things away, slowly settled back into their seats and waited. It was always a mixture of excitement, fear and hope. Sometimes, Mrs Cresswell would say "Guess what, no homework this week", but rarely. The class waited.

"Well," said Mrs Cresswell with a smile, "there is homework this week." A good-hearted, quiet jeer went round the room. "Now, now," Mrs Cresswell said, "I think you might like this! I would like you to think about something you are proud of. It can be anything at all, but it must make you proud. And you can decide what it feels like to be proud. I will choose three people to read out their work, because we won't have time for everyone to read theirs, and the rest can just hand it in. We shall pick the names out of the pot on Monday morning, and you can read them at the end of the day, to give you time to prepare."

Stella was quite happy with this as a homework task because she knew straight away what she would talk about. She knew what she was most proud of. Over the weekend she wrote what she was going to say. She thought she probably wouldn't get chosen from the pot. She always got nervous when she had to speak in front of the class, but she kind of wanted to tell her story to everyone because it was something she really believed in.

The weekend flashed by as they usually do, and as she lay in bed on Sunday night, she still wasn't sure if she wanted to get picked to read out her homework the next day. She still didn't know as she walked into school and she still didn't know as Mrs Cresswell held the pot and said, "Well, everyone. I hope you have all done your homework and have it ready to hand in." She looked at Tommy as she said this because she knew that there was very little chance that Tommy would have done his homework. He looked down at his table.

"OK, let's see who is going to be speaking to us this afternoon." Mrs Cresswell picked a lolly stick out of the jar. She looked at it and smiled. "Clint! You're going to be the first."

There was a mumble of excitement. Clint was a popular lad. His family were very rich and lived in an enormous house at the edge of the town.

Mrs Cresswell smiled, "I'm sure that we will enjoy hearing what you are proud of." Clint smiled and looked pleased that he had been picked. "Right then, let's see who is next."

Stella thought "Oh wow, I bet Clint has lots he is proud of," and suddenly thought her presentation would not be exciting enough, and now she hoped she wasn't picked.

The class fell silent as Mrs Cresswell hung her fingers over the lolly-lotto jar. Her bright red fingernails picked up a second lolly stick. "Noosha, It's you." There was a little cheer. Noosha was very popular and was fantastic at all sports. The children could imagine what she was going to talk about. Stella was now desperate that she wasn't the next name pulled out because she knew that Clint would have lots of things to be proud of, and Noosha would have all her sporting achievements. She was now sitting, scared, as Mrs Cresswell went to the jar again.

"And the third person is…" There was a pause like you see on TV when the 'public have voted', then the nails went in again. They grabbed a lolly stick and Mrs Cresswell announced, "Stella." Stella's heart jumped – she was scared, excited and felt sick all at the same time. "So, we have Clint, Noosha and Stella. I'm sure they all have a lot to be proud about. You can spend some time this afternoon planning your talks."

After lunch all three children did some planning, and quickly the time arrived for them to deliver their talks. The class sat around in their usual positions. Stella had a wobbly feeling in her tummy about talking in front of the class. She was partly happy about being able to tell her classmates what she was proud of, but she was scared. She was also worried that Clint and Noosha would have more exciting things to talk about. Stella thought she would just have to "get on with it," as her grandma would say. Grandma also said, "the things you enjoy the most are usually scary."

First up was Clint. Clint had made a PowerPoint presentation, and the whiteboard said: Being Clint - I'm so proud!

He stood up and spoke. "Hi everyone, as you know I am Clint, and I am very proud of lots of things. Firstly, I am proud of my house." He clicked the clicker, and a picture of his beautiful house came up.

"Wow!" everyone said, as they looked at the fabulous house.

"It has 12 bedrooms."

"Wow!" they all said.

"A stable block with ten horses." He clicked and a picture appeared of the stables with beautiful horses.

"Wow!"

"A 20-metre pool," another picture.

"Wow!"

"And a tennis court."

He went through all the things his lovely house had. Stella felt more sick.

After describing the wonderful house, Clint told the class how proud he was of the cars his family had. There was a Lamborghini, a Porsche, and a huge Mercedes. There were "wows" every time he clicked on a new slide. After talking about the cars, he told the class how proud he was of his family holiday home in the Cayman Islands, showing pictures. And then finally, he talked about how proud he was of his, yes, *his*, motorbike which he was allowed to drive around the grounds of the house, even though he was only ten.

After about ten minutes, he ended his presentation, and everyone cheered and clapped. Stella did too, but inside she still felt very sick. "Well done, Clint, gosh you are a lucky boy," said Mrs Cresswell. "Right, your turn Noosha."

Noosha stood up. She was confident and started straight away, talking about how proud she was of her sporting achievements. She had got the school office to ring home when she knew she was going to be talking and her mum had brought in a big case full of bright shiny trophies and cups. "This is a trophy I won when I was the county champion at badminton," she said, holding up the beautiful silver trophy.

"Wow!" the class said when they saw it.

"That's so cool," shouted Tommy - it was the first time Stella had ever heard him say anything. He was right, it was cool.

Noosha explained how she was the county champion at squash and cross-country as well and had been signed by Leeds United's football academy. She described how she had won most of the cups and trophies, and there were lots and lots of wows! At the end, she thanked them for listening and sat down. There was a big round of applause and a bit of cheering. Stella clapped and cheered too, but now she knew it was her turn.

"Right Stella, your turn now." Mrs Cresswell smiled at her, and Stella rose to her feet.

"Hello, I'm Stella, I'm sorry, but I don't have a PowerPoint or anything to show you like Clint and Noosha had. I want to tell you about the thing I am most proud of, it's my family. There was no sound, no wowing, but why would there be, thought Stella. The class was sitting perfectly nicely, listening.

"Mum and Dad came to the country from Jamaica 25 years ago. They didn't have much money and they didn't know anyone. They got jobs which they didn't really like, but they knew that they had to work hard and that if they worked hard, they could do well. They worked really hard and earned enough money to save a bit. After a while they had saved enough to buy a tiny house, not as big and posh as Clint's house, but a nice house all the same.

Then, when they had enough money, they started a family. They had my brother and me. I am proud because my mum and dad have worked so hard and given my brother and me a good life and a nice place to live. I am proud that my family is from Jamaica, because it's a beautiful island; lots of people from this country save up to go there for their holidays. I am proud to be born in Britain but have Jamaican heritage.

I am proud of my brother because he isn't well; he has an illness which makes it hard for him to breathe, but he just gets on with life. He never moans, he is funny, and he makes me laugh, and lastly, I am proud of my Gran. She still lives in Jamaica, and she is 80 now, but she has learned to use an iPad so we can FaceTime with her every week. She is great! She tells me stories about Jamaica and makes fun of how cold the weather is in Britain and how sunny it is in Jamaica." As she spoke a tear ran down Stella's face, not because she was sad but because she really was proud when she thought of her amazing family. "Anyway," she said, "that's my family and I am very, very proud of them."

There had been no wows at all, but when she finished the children stood up and cheered. Stella's pride had been so strong that the children not only enjoyed her talk, but they were also proud of their classmate. Clint and Noosha stood and cheered too, and Noosha even hugged Sella.

Mrs Cresswell thanked all three of the children who spoke and said "It's lovely to be proud of what you have like Clint, and well-done Clint. And to be proud of what you have done and achieved; you have done and achieved lots Noosha, very well done. But I think we could all see how wonderful it is to be proud of who you are and where you and your family have come from. We could all see how proud you are Stella!" The class cheered again, and that night Stella video called her Gran to tell her all about how she was even more proud now.

# A MATTER OF PRIDE

This is the story of a girl who is asked to speak to her class about something of which she is proud. Whilst others talk about what they have or have done, she talks about where she is from, her heritage and her family.

The themes are:

- How precious family is.
- Being proud of heritage and family history.
- The true value of who you are.

### Story map.

- Stella and her class are set weekend homework to write about something of which they are proud.
- They are told that three of them will be chosen to present their work to the rest of the class.
- Stella does not like talking to the whole class but enjoys the work as it really makes her think, and she is very proud.
- Mrs Cresswell, their teacher picks out the names of the children who will present their work in the afternoon. Clint, Noosha and Stella (who is very nervous).
- The three get time to prepare in the afternoon.
- Clint has a PowerPoint showing huge houses, flash cars and amazing holidays, each of which he is very proud. Everyone 'wows' at each of the slides and cheers and claps at the end.
- Noosha has rung home, and her mum has brought a big suitcase full of trophies that she is proud of, and she talks about all of her incredible sporting achievements.

The children all wow at each trophy and clap and cheer at the end.
- ➢ Stella has no PowerPoint or trophies to show but she talks about her family and how proud she is.
- ➢ Her parents who moved to the UK and made a good life for them all,
- ➢ Her brother who is ill but is cheerful and never complains.
- ➢ Her grandma who still lives in Jamaica and is very old but has learned to use an iPad to see them all and talks with them ever week.
- ➢ She is also proud of her Jamaican heritage and proud to be from the UK.
- ➢ The children all sit and listen with no wows, but they see her pride and at the end give the loudest cheer and clap and Noosha hugs Stella.
- ➢ Mrs Cresswell thanks all three but says that Stella has shown them that sometimes it's just as important to be proud of who you are and where you are from.

# Greedy Town

Once, there was a town in a country which might have been near here, or it might have been a long way away; it does not really matter. The thing about this town was that the people were too bothered about things. If a new gadget, phone, computer or car was released, there would be a race to be the first in the town to have it. Everyone wanted the biggest and best house. Everyone wanted to go on the most expensive holidays, own the most unusual and exotic pets, and have the flashiest watch, the largest television and the most exclusive designer clothes and jewellery. Anyone who moved to the town who didn't have such expensive things soon felt uncomfortable and rarely stayed long. It was not a friendly town, because everyone was always nervous about not having the best things.

One day, posters appeared all over the town. The posters said:

'WHO HAS THE MOST VALUABLE THING IN TOWN?'

They said that a competition was going to be held the following Saturday at 7:30pm, at St Michael's Hall in the high street. They said that people should bring the most valuable thing they had, and a panel of judges would declare what was the most precious and impressive item in the town.

Everyone was instantly very excited and started to think about what they would bring. The people were all very suspicious, and they stopped talking to each other. Parents told their children not to speak to their friends in case they gave away secrets about what their family was going to take to the competition. It was all that the town could think about. It was the biggest thing ever to have happened and it took the levels of jealousy, greed and unfriendliness to new heights.

When the big day arrived, it was a cold but bright morning. At first, the streets were empty, a few sparrows and occasional people walking their expensive pedigree dogs were all that moved. Everyone was preparing for the competition. People were polishing jewels, dusting masterpiece paintings, shining vintage cars and counting gold bars. The only thing which was heard was the sound of armour-plated security vans moving into place to collect the treasures, which each person hoped would prove that they were the richest, and therefore, in their eyes, the best person in the town.

By 7pm the vans were queueing up outside St Michael's Hall, each carefully unloading its precious cargo, with everything being covered so that no one knew what was being offered as the most valuable thing in the town of valuable things.

As the old St Michael's Hall clock clunked round to 7:30, all was set. Each person would take it in turn to explain what they had brought and why it was so valuable. Everyone stared suspiciously at one another as they stood next to their various, sheet-covered objects, some enormous, others small, but all very precious.

Well, actually that's not entirely true. There was one man, a stranger, who just stood there alone. He wasn't beside anything. No one knew who he was, but they all wondered what he had brought. Most presumed that he must have a massive jewel in his pocket or maybe a letter from William Shakespeare or some other small but priceless object.

The first to go was General Peregrine Spofforth-Smedlington. No one was sure which army he had been a general of, but he was very posh, rich and full of self-importance. He stood next to a strangely shaped canvas-covered lump. As he pulled the canvas away it revealed a staggering sight. A solid gold canon, it had wheels which were encrusted with jewels and looked like something from Aladdin's cave. The General looked very pleased with himself, cleared his throat and introduced his entry to the competition. "This is the 'Aczan Canon', it is solid gold and was used to fire the last shot of a war between two great kings. I took it after we were victorious in that war." The people in the hall were clearly impressed; it was undoubtedly a very magnificent item.

The next person to show their most valuable possession was Mickey Steel. He was a retired rock star and lived in a massive house on the edge of the town. He was tall and very thin, with long, straggly, suspiciously black hair which dangled from a peaked cap. He had what was a clearly guitar-shaped item under his sheet. He pulled the sheet off and then explained what it was. "This is *the* guitar. It was used by Lenny Bragg, the greatest rock star ever known. It was used to play the guitar solos on many of the biggest hits in the seventies and eighties. It is a Gibson Les Paul Sunburst and is completely priceless in the world of rock music. I paid 10 million pounds for it in an auction in New York last year, but I have been offered ten times that amount since." There was a buzz of excitement and a few people clapped. Everyone was getting more excited. Everyone apart from the stranger, who just seemed to watch.

Mrs Jenkins was a fairly large lady in a green dress. She had a string of enormous pearls around her neck, and dangly earrings which gave her the look of a Christmas tree. Her husband had suddenly died, some time ago. There was a lot of talk in the town that his death might not have been an accident, and that Mrs Jenkins might not be the innocent widow she liked people to think she was. Her item was small, and most people knew what it was. She pulled away the cover from the table-top exhibit. There, as everyone expected, was the Jenkins' Diamond, thought of as the third largest diamond in the world and the biggest which wasn't in a royal crown somewhere. "As you know, this is the Jenkins' Diamond. It has been in my late husband's family for two hundred years." She stopped, to appear upset at the thought of her husband. She continued, "the stone is perfect in colour, cut and clarity. It was recently valued at twenty-three million pounds by Sotheby's in London." People pushed forward to see the jewel, but the stranger seemed to be watching the people of the town rather than their priceless possessions.

And so it continued. Each of the rich inhabitants, in turn, showed something which created an array of items which would have made the top museums and galleries in the world jealous. Dr Owen had a signed first edition of Romeo and Juliet, Mr and Mrs Gullstrapper had brought the football with which England had won the World Cup. The Bush family simply brought a massive treasure chest full of gold, and on it went for three hours, until it came to the stranger who was the last person to show what he had brought. Everyone was very interested to hear what he was going to say and, more importantly, see what he was going to show.

He stepped forward, but before he could speak all the lights went out and the whole hall was cast into absolute darkness. There were one or two screams, but the darkness only lasted a few seconds before all the lights came on again, much brighter than before, and it was soon clear that some extra people were in the hall. At the top of a staircase, which led to a storeroom, was a tall man, and he had a gun. Not an antique solid gold gun, but a modern, very dangerous-looking machine gun.

He introduced himself. "Ladies and gentlemen," he shouted, and to make certain he had everyone's attention, he fired his gun into the air. "Thank you so much for coming here tonight. Oh, and please can we save you some time? We have put an induction coil around the hall and so your mobile phones are completely useless. This, as you may have realised, is a robbery." Mrs Jenkins fainted.

"My colleagues and I will now relieve you of these marvellous treasures," the man continued, "which you have been kind enough to bring along tonight." He pointed around the hall where now stood dark figures, each carrying a similar gun to the man who had spoken. He was clearly the leader. He continued. "We were planning to rob each of you at home, but we thought you would all have state-of-the-art security systems and alarms, which would have made our lives very difficult. We realised that the thing which would help us was the fact that you people are show-offs, and need to think you have better, more expensive things than your neighbours. You are ridiculous, and need to realise that your worth is not measured by what you have but by who you are. Having said that, your stupidity has made our lives much easier." With that, the thieves went round collecting the valuable things and taking them to their vans, which were waiting outside.

The people of the town sat stunned, some crying quietly, a few trying to resuscitate Mrs Jenkins, all were in shock. Before long, the robbers had closed their vans' doors and driven away. The stranger had not moved or spoken, apart from having a brief conversation with one of the robbers, who quickly left him alone. Mickey Steele suddenly moved towards him.

"Oi! Who are you? Are you in on this? How come they took nothing off you?" The town's folk turned accusingly towards the stranger, demanding to know what was going on. At last, the stranger spoke.

"Well, I'm new to the town. I didn't realise that you must have expensive things to get on here. I did bring my most precious things with me, but they were of no use to the robbers. "Here, look." He took out some photographs. "These are pictures of my family. Unfortunately, my Mum and Dad are both dead now and these are all I have to remind me of them. I also have pictures of my children, who I don't see often because I'm away from them, working near here. My memories of my parents and my love for my family are far more valuable to me than any painting, cannon, diamond or guitar. I feel sorry for you. You have had things taken, but I feel even more sorry for you because you don't realise that the truly valuable things in life are not things which you buy in jewellers' shops or at auctions."

With that, he turned and walked away, leaving the people of the town to reflect on what was valuable and what was not.

# **GREEDY TOWN**

The story of a town where the possessions you own are a measure of your worth as a person. Where people want to show off how rich they are. This helps a gang of armed robbers to trick them and steal their possessions. Except one man who is new and whose most treasured possessions are photos of his family.

The themes are:

- Greed can consume you.
- There are more important things than wealth.
- Memories are precious.

## **Story map**

> There is a town where everyone is a show-off. They are only bothered about what they have and how other people see them.
> They think that their worth is only really measured by how expensive their possessions are.
> One day posters are put up saying a big competition is to be held to see who has the most valuable possession in the town.
> The people start to prepare and build towards the big day.
> They all take their very valuable things to the hall and take it in turn to tell everyone else about their incredibly expensive and valuable things; guitars, cannons, jewels etc.
> There is one stranger who looks on in silence. No one knows who he is.

- He is the last person to 'show and tell' but just as he is about speak, armed robbers turn very bright lights on and tell the people they are about to be robbed. The people cannot get out or use their phones as they have put something round the hall which has jammed the signal.
- The robbers load their vans and then leave the people devastated about their treasure being taken.
- The people turn on the stranger and accuse him of being involved and want to know what his valuable possession is.
- He explains that he has brought some photographs of his family. He takes them out of his jacket pocket and explains why they are so precious.
- He says that he does not measure value just in money and that he feels sorry for them because they have been robbed, but he feels more sorry for them because they do not really understand the meaning of the word valuable.

# **Derek and the Optimist**

Derek did not really know what he was, but whatever he was, he didn't like it. He was a greeny-brown colour and about three centimetres long. He didn't do much apart from eat, and all he ever ate was leaves.

He couldn't remember being born (well, who can?!) and he didn't know what life was really all about. All he knew was that he just had this real urge to keep eating leaves. There were a lot of other creatures like Derek and most of them never spoke; they just kept their heads down and ate leaves.

Derek thought he was very, very unlucky to have been born a… whatever he was. He saw other animals and wished he was them. There were some who could fly; birds of course, but Derek didn't know what we call them! There were some that could travel really quickly; that was almost every other animal when compared with Derek, who was tiny and whose legs were even tinier. There was one who could dig gigantic holes; that was a mole. There were lots of other creatures, all of which seemed to have much more interesting and fulfilling lives than Derek and the others of his kind.

There was one other of Derek's kind who he did speak to, or more accurately who spoke to Derek. Derek didn't know his name, but he was very optimistic. Derek was talking one day about how boring life was, just eating leaves all the time, but the other creature said, "Well, at least we have got something to eat, we will not starve, and you never know when things are going to get better. It might be in a minute, it might be in an hour, or it might be in a week or even a year, but I am sure that they will get better!"

Derek didn't really believe that things would get better, not in a week or a year or ever. He was just a squidgy grub who ate leaves. The only way things would probably change would be when, one day, one of the flying animals (the birds) would come and eat him, because that happened from time to time. Derek always made sure he was under the leaf he was eating because he had noticed that those of his kind which ate on top of the leaf got eaten themselves.

One day, Derek and the optimistic one were eating near each other and a bird swooped down and gobbled up one of the others from the top of the leaf Derek was nibbling. "That's awful! I really dislike being one of us, I don't want to get eaten," he cried.

"Oh well, at least it was quick," said the optimist, "she wouldn't have felt a thing and at least she provided that creature with a meal… and you never know when things are going to get better. It might be in a minute, it might be in an hour, or it might be in a week or even a year, but I am sure that they will get better!'

"Well, I can't see a way they are going to get better!" said Derek.

One afternoon, one of the people who owned the garden where Derek lived was mowing the lawn. They mowed right over the place where Derek, the optimist and some others were eating leaves. As the mower went over them, they got thrown high into the air with all the grass cuttings. They were very lucky because they didn't get chopped up, but they easily could have been. Derek felt sick.

"Argh! That was awful, we could have been chopped up and I feel dreadful being thrown in the air like that. I landed on my head, and I have a headache now!" He was very cross, but of course the optimist wasn't cross.

"Well, I think we should be grateful we *weren't* chopped up, not angry... and you never know when things are going to get better. It might be in a minute, it might be in an hour, or it might be in a week or even a year, but I am sure that they will get better!'

These occasional near-disasters were the only way life was interesting or different. Every day, all Derek and the others did was eat leaves. Whenever something happened which upset Derek and made him even more fed up with being a... whatever he was, the optimistic creature would say that it wasn't that bad and, "you never know when things are going to get better. It might be in a minute, it might be in an hour, or it might be in a week or even a year, but I am sure that they will get better!"

Derek sometimes thought it was quite funny, the way the other creature was always so positive, and sometimes it just got on his nerves.

One day, Derek didn't feel very well. Well, at least he thought he didn't. He had never been ill, so he didn't really know, but he certainly felt strange. For one thing, he suddenly didn't want to eat any more. All of his life, he could only remember just wanting to eat, but now, he didn't. In fact, the thought of eating made him feel sick. He also felt exhausted. He tried to walk but he couldn't, so he just lay down. Derek thought this was it, he was dying. He thought what a pointless and dull life he had had. He was just about to close his eyes when he saw the optimist, who also was feeling ill and also no longer felt like eating.

"See," said Derek, "you see, we're finished. Our lives got no better, did they? We were just leaf eaters."

"Oh, don't be like that," said the weak optimist, "we don't know what's happening and as I have always said, you never know when things are going to get better. It might be in a minute, it might be in an hour, or it might be in a week or even a year, but I am sure that they will get better!"

Derek was too weak to say what he wanted to, and then he couldn't see or hear anything as he lay there, still and silent.

Suddenly, Derek woke up. He didn't know where he was. "Am I dead?" he thought to himself and then decided that he probably wasn't, although he really didn't know what that would feel like. He felt as if he was in a tube. He thought that maybe he had been so ill he had fallen inside something. He wriggled and squirmed to get out. Moving was strange, and he felt very odd indeed.

It took him ages to wriggle out of whatever it was he was in. The bright light hit his eyes; he couldn't see properly at first, everything was blurred, but he could hear. The first thing he heard was the optimist, who sounded very cheerful. "See," said the optimist, "I told you, didn't I?"

"What, told me what?" asked Derek, still very confused and still not able to see properly.

"I told you things would get better!"

"Well, I can't really see how things are any better, I seem unable to move properly and… oh." At that moment Derek could suddenly see clearly. He could see the optimist, or at least he thought it was him, but it didn't look like him. Instead of being greeny-brown, he was red and orange and yellow. And he was much bigger, or at least he looked it, because he now had things like the flying animals had, and they were spread out.

The optimist had become a butterfly! (Although of course Derek didn't know that that is what we call them). "Wow," said Derek, "look at you! You look fantastic!" Then, feeling jealous, he said, "You lucky thing!"

"Haha," laughed the beautiful butterfly, "not lucky me! Lucky us, look at yourself!"

Derek looked down at himself. It was incredible. He looked just like the optimist, except his wings were still curled up. He stretched them out, and they unfurled. They were just as beautiful, and soon they were ready to use. Neither of them knew how, but they managed to fly and now they had the urge to eat again. But not leaves this time; now they had the urge to drink from some beautiful flowers and the drink tasted sweet and wonderful. Derek was so happy. Things certainly had got much, much better. "It just goes to show you," he said to his friend. "You never know when things are going to get better, it might be in a minute, it might be in an hour or it might be in a week or even a year, but they can get better!"

# **DEREK AND THE OPTIMIST**

This is the tale of Derek, a miserable caterpillar who does not know what lies ahead, and his friend who keeps telling him that things will be ok and that you never know when things will get better. Eventually they do.

The themes are:

- Keep positive.
- You never know what lies ahead.
- Things can change.

## **Story map**

- ➢ Derek does not know what he is.
- ➢ He is a podgy little grub and does not like it because all he does is eat leaves.
- ➢ There are lots of others; most don't speak, but one is chatty and cheerful.
- ➢ He always says things will change, "it might be in a minute, it might be in an hour, in a week or even a year", but he is always sure things will change.
- ➢ Derek, the optimist and the other grubs have various scrapes, with a lawn mower and some hungry birds, and Derek gets more upset and miserable, but the optimist stays positive, saying his mantra: "It might be in a minute, it might be in an hour, in a week or even a year."
- ➢ But things don't change until one day when Derek feels strange and for the first time in his life does not feel like

- eating. He thinks he is dying and thinks his life has been a waste of time.
- Suddenly Derek wakes up and can hear the optimist, who is happy. Then he sees him.
- He has turned into a beautiful butterfly. At first, Derek is jealous but then the optimist points out that Derek is the same and he should uncurl his wings.
- Derek does this and they fly away together to drink sweet nectar from flowers.

# The Strangely Strong Weakling

The jungle was a noisy place, with monkeys chattering in the trees and birds flying high and calling to their friends. The fast-flowing river thundered through the valley, and you could hear the occasional sound of a truck bumping along the rough road, which humans had made by chopping down a line of trees.

In one part of the jungle, the animals all got on well. They lived respectful lives and went about their business. Well, all the animals apart from Drac, that is. Drac wasn't respectful at all. Drac was a silverback gorilla and was bigger and stronger than all the other animals, and he thought this made him special.

He bossed the other creatures around, telling them that if they didn't do as he commanded, they would get hurt. And they often did get hurt. Drac was not a very nice animal; he behaved in a bullying way. He didn't have any friends, and those animals which hung around with him did so because they feared him. Most animals just tried to keep out of his way.

Drac suffered from being too proud to let any other animal think he was wrong, scared or weak, in any way. He would never, ever let any other creature get the better of him and anyone he thought was a threat, he would chase away.

The most dangerous place to meet Drac was 'fallen tree bridge', which was where a tree had fallen down and made a bridge across a very narrow part of the river. The tree was quite dangerous, even when Drac wasn't on it. It was twisted and bumpy and some bits were shiny and slippery. Because it was so narrow at this point, the river was deep, fast-flowing, and extremely dangerous. The tree was not very wide and because of this, Drac would get furious and aggressive if any other animal was using it when he wanted to cross. No other animal wanted to be on the bridge with Drac as they knew he would happily throw them off, into the raging river below.

One day, a strange new animal arrived in the jungle. The other animals were curious about her. They had never seen an animal like her before. She was obviously some kind of rat, but not like the rats who lived in the jungle. She was tiny, and weak looking, but seemed friendly enough.

"Hi y'all, my name is Mary-Lou," she said, in an accent the others didn't recognise.

"Hello," said a squirrel, "I haven't seen you round here before."

"Gee, that's right. That's because I haven't been round these parts before. I just got here," the friendly newcomer said.

"But where did you come from?" asked a chimpanzee.

"Well, it's a funny story," the stranger continued, "I used to live in a zoo with human beings staring at me all day. It was OK but very boring. Anyhow, I got transferred to another zoo, and I was in a cage on the back of a truck, along with some other animals. The truck hit a great big hole in the road, and my cage got thrown off and it smashed apart when it landed at the side of the road. It shook me up but not too bad, so I guess I escaped. And here I am!"

"Wow! That's so cool," said a parrot, "are you going to stay here?"

"I guess so, for a while anyhow. You guys seem swell!"

So, the strange, skinny rat-like creature stayed, and she was happy in the jungle community. Then, one day, when she was chatting to some monkeys near the river, they all heard a booming, threatening voice. "Get out of my way, you pathetic weaklings. Unless you want to feel a lot of pain, I suggest you get right out of my way... Now!" It was Drac, of course. It was the first time Mary-Lou had come into contact with the gorilla. She had heard about him, but not yet seen him. She asked what the problem was.

"Oh, he is horrible at the best of times, but when others are crossing the bridge, he is just dreadful. He gets even more angry. It's best to just let him have his own way and live in peace," a monkey explained.

"But doesn't anyone tell him to wait his turn?" Mary-Lou asked.

The other animals laughed. "That would be like saying: 'Excuse me Drac, could you throw me in the river?', because that's what he would do." They all chuckled at the thought of telling Drac to wait his turn.

But Mary-Lou wasn't happy about the way Drac thought he could have what he wanted, because he was bigger and stronger than everyone else. She decided to do something about it!

It was an incredibly hot day, even by African jungle standards. The sun was like a big angry orange in the bright blue sky. The heat wriggled off the rocks in a haze that made things look like a dream. Mary-Lou didn't mind; in fact, she was glad it was so hot.

She waited by the bridge until she could hear the snarling and growling of Drac, ordering the other animals out of the way. As he got near to the bridge, Mary-Lou hopped on to the other end and started to cross. Drac spotted her straight away. "Oi, you, rat thing, get out of my way. Can't you see I'm crossing!?"

"Well, of course I can see that, but the thing is, I was on the bridge first, so I think the fair thing to do is for you to back up and let me cross. Don't you?"

"What!? No, I don't think that! I think you have three seconds to get off this bridge or you will be flying into that river down there, with your next stop the sea!" Drac was booming, snarling and very, very angry. He did not really like being on the bridge. He was an enormous animal, and he didn't feel very stable when he was on the slippery tree trunk. Of course, he would let no-one else know this. By now, a big crowd of animals had gathered at each end of the bridge. They were very pleased to see someone standing up to Drac but felt bad because they were all pretty sure that Mary-Lou was very close to being badly hurt.

"Well, the thing is, Drac- it is Drac, isn't it? – I'm Mary-Lou by the way."

"I don't care who you are, just get out of my way. NOW!" snarled the silverback.

"Well, as I was saying," Mary-Lou calmly continued, "the thing is, I'm a rat and have tiny feet and legs and weigh very little so I'm really steady when I'm on this bridge." She did a little dance to prove her point. "You, on the other hand, are a great big lump of a creature and not at all stable on here, are you? I reckon if you grab at me, I will be able to move out of the way, and you might just fall into that very fast river down there. If I try to get past you, I shall undoubtedly be in big trouble, so I think I shall just wait here. It is very hot though, eh?"

It was very hot, and Drac was feeling it under his fur. "Just get out of my way!" he repeated, although now he was sounding a bit desperate. He knew that the rat was right, and he could not risk grabbing at her because he might fall. He had never been in this situation before, so he just stood there in the hot, hot sun with an ever-increasing crowd of animals watching on, as the skinny Mary-Lou stood up to the massive Drac. And all the time the sun was beating down.

"Look," said Drac, "you've made your point, now come on, move out of my way and I will just hurt you a bit." The other animals had never heard Drac talk like this before. He seemed weak; the sun was obviously having an effect.

"No. Like I said," Mary-Lou replied, "I was on this bridge first and it's only fair that you back up and let me cross!"

"Never!" shouted the increasingly desperate gorilla. "Get out of my way now!" As he screamed this command, his legs buckled under him, and he fell forward. The creatures at either end of the bridge gasped; they could not believe their eyes. He repositioned his feet, but the sun had sapped his strength and he nearly fell. There was silence as all the other animals just watched, not knowing what was going to happen next. Drac was horrible, but he wasn't stupid, and he knew that he was weak from the heat of the midday sun. He had to end this. He made a grab for Mary-Lou. She simply skipped out of the way. Drac was now wobbling. He tried again to regain his balance, but this time it was no good. His knees buckled, and slowly the great ape toppled off the fallen tree. There was silence from each end of the bridge, then Drac splashed into the fast-flowing river which carried him far away from the animals and the bridge.

A tremendous cheer echoed round the jungle, with whooping and general happiness coming from all the other animals. Mary-Lou walked triumphantly across the bridge and the other animals crowded round her, patting her on the back, clapping and shouting. When the excitement had died down a little, her friend, the squirrel, came forward and said, "Well done, Mary-Lou. But how did you know you would win? What if the sun had got to you before it got to Drac?"

"Well," Mary-Lou started, "you always must use your own strengths. Drac's special strengths are his muscles and size. I couldn't possibly win if we were fighting using muscles and size, so I had to use my special talent. Once I did that, I was fairly sure I would win. You see, in the part of the United States where I'm from, it gets mighty hot and us Kangaroo Rats have developed a way of living there. We are adapted for living in the desert. We don't even need to drink, we can get water from our food, so you see this wasn't really very hard for me. Poor old Drac never really stood a chance because he couldn't use his special talent, and I could use mine."

Drac was washed far downstream and eventually crawled out of the water to start a new life in another part of the jungle. He told no one there about how he had been beaten by a little rat, but now he showed greater respect to other animals and no longer thought that because he was big and strong, he was the best. And guess what? He was a happier gorilla because of it!

# THE STRANGELY STRONG WEAKLING

When a strange new animal arrives in the jungle, she shows the other animals that if you play to your strengths, you can stand up to those who try to use aggression and threats to push you around.

The themes are:

- Don't let others push you around.
- There are strengths other than muscles.
- You might not know what you are dealing with.
- Think of your own strengths and use them.

**Story map**

- Drac is a big and unpleasant gorilla who thinks because he is big and strong, he can have what he wants.
- A strange rat-like creature (Mary-Lou) arrives in the jungle, having escaped from a zoo.
- The other animals are friendly and warn her about Drac and she hears about Drac being a bully many times.
- One very hot day Drac wants to cross 'fallen tree bridge' but Mary-Lou is already on the bridge.
- Mary-Lou points out that Drac is a bit wobbly, and she is small and nimble, and he dare not attack her on the bridge.
- Drac threatens and shouts, but Mary-Lou stands her ground.
- They have a standoff in the scorching hot sun.
- The animals watch aghast.

- Eventually the heat gets to Drac, and his knees buckle, and he falls into the river below, which carries him off far downstream.
- Mary-Lou is mobbed by the other animals. She tells the other animals that she is a Kangaroo rat from America and is specially adapted for surviving very hot and dry conditions, so she knew the heat would hurt Drac much more than it would hurt her. He never stood a chance.

# The Creature in the Shell

Gina lived by the sea, in a seaside town called Scarby. It was the sort of place that was great for a day out, or even for a family holiday. The houses were all painted bright colours and seagulls shouted down at the people below, always looking for chips to steal. There was a funfair, an amusement park and a pier which stuck out into the sea like a finger pointing at the ships which slid across the horizon. During the long summer holidays, Gina, who was ten, liked to watch the visitors who had come to enjoy themselves. She thought it was funny that they would sit for hours in traffic jams to get to the seaside, which for her was just at the bottom of the street.

One day, Gina was sitting on the wall at the bottom of her garden. It was her favourite place to people-watch. A large man caught her eye. He was staring at a seashell. He was enormous with thick arms and a neck which made him look like he could easily carry a car on his head. He stared hard at the shell, as though he was trying to look right through it. He was concentrating on the shell so much he didn't notice his friends returning from the fish and chip shop. "What you doing?" said one friend, another big chap with a bald head and a hat stuck on top of it that said, 'Kiss Me Quick!' He handed the first man his fish and chips.

"I just saw a really strange little animal go into this shell. I have seen nothing like it before, I really haven't," said the huge man.

The third man, who had a vast amount of red hair and a very bushy beard, which made him look like his head could go on either way up, suddenly looked very excited. He grunted and rushed back to the fish and chip shop. When he was inside, he tore down a poster which was pinned to a notice board. He didn't seem to mind that it was a rude thing to do.

The poster said that the local museum, along with museums around the country, was linking up with the Natural History Museum in London to find new species of animals. If anyone could send in a photo, and it was confirmed as a brand-new species which no one else had ever found, then they might win £10,000. As soon as the other two men saw the poster, they got very excited too.

"Ten grand!" squealed the first man, "and it will all be mine!"

"We're gonna share it, aren't we?" said the man with the beard, scratching him bottom.

"Yeah, we gotta share," the kiss me quick man said, picking his nose.

"Well, we gotta get it out first, then we can decide what we do with the cash," the first man said. That was rather sensible for these three, thought Gina; she was loving watching them, it was hilarious.

The three friends stood there, eating their fish and chips, looking at the shell and hoping that the strange little animal would simply come out. They all had their phones ready to take a picture if it stuck its head, or any other bit, out of the shell. They finished their food and their cans of cola, the animal was still happily inside.

"Well, what do you think then? How are we gonna get the creature out?" asked the first man, eventually.

"I have an idea," said the kiss me quick man.

Gina thought, "his should be good."

"It might understand English, so just tell it to come out. Our dog will do as it is told, so this creature might do as well." He picked up the shell and shouted at it. "Oi, little animal, come out!" The animal stayed where it was. "Come on, come on, get out of there, come on!" Try as he might, the rather dim, large man failed miserably to get the creature to emerge from the safety of the shell. "Well, I don't know how to get it out. You try." He tossed the shell to his hairy friend.

Up stepped the second of the men, licking his chippy fingers and wiping his hands on his jeans. "Give us it 'ere," he instructed. He peered into the shell. "If it won't come out when asked nicely, we will have to be a bit more forceful. Come out you silly little thing!" He shouted into the shell, "Out you come, now... or, or, or you'll be sorry!" In the shell the little creature just crawled further down; there was no way it was leaving the shell with all that noise going on outside.

The first man stepped forward. He had a bit of fish hanging from his mouth now and spoke as if he was in charge. "Gimme it 'ere" he told the beardy man. "If it won't understand simple instructions, then maybe it will need more than words. With that he shook the shell as if it were a tomato ketchup bottle, with particularly thick sauce in it. He shook it every way possible and quite hard, but the creature inside just squeezed itself further into the shell. It was actually quite comfortable. Eventually, the man stopped shaking the shell and tossed it into the flowerbed at the side of the road, between the path and the beach. "I give up."

"We could just smash the shell up," said hat man.

"Nah, look, it says here it has to be alive," said beardy, pointing at the poster.

"Ah well," said the hat man, "probably wasn't even a rare animal, anyway!" And with that, the three friends went off to find something else to amuse themselves with.

Gina had enjoyed watching the rather silly men trying to talk, shout, and then finally shake the poor animal out of its shell. She decided to have an ice cream. When she had nearly finished, she walked over to the place where she had seen the men drop the shell. She picked it up and put it on the concrete floor. She broke off a piece of her ice cream cone and placed it in front of the shell. She stepped back and got her phone ready to take the picture. Moments later, the little creature came carefully out of its hiding place and ate the ice cream cone. Gina took lots and lots of photographs, from every angle. She also took a picture of the poster the men had left in the road. It had the museum's website and contact details on it. As soon as she got home, she wrote a message to the museum and attached the photos.

Time passed, and Gina had pretty much forgotten about the little creature. Then, one day, her parents received a phone call congratulating them and saying that their daughter had discovered a brand new species of sea creature and saying that she would get £10,000 which would be presented in London, at a special event at the Natural History Museum.

It was big news in the town and the local paper interviewed Gina. At the big presentation event, they asked her if it had been hard to get the animal out of its shell, to which she answered: "Well, I thought the best way to get something or someone to do what you want is to be kind to them. It's funny how we often call animals dumb, but I can think of a few humans who might fit that description better." She smiled to herself and collected the huge cheque.

# **THE CREATURE IN THE SHELL**

This is a story about trying to get a little animal out of its shell. Some big, silly men try to scare, shake, and just demand it out. A little girl, who has been watching, shows that giving the creature a reason to come out and a sense of security is much more effective.

The themes are:

- Winning someone over is more effective than forcing them.
- Being threatening might not get you what you want.
- Being aggressive can make you seem silly.

## **Story map**

- Gina lives at the seaside and likes to watch the tourists who visit.
- One day she is watching three big and not very clever men.
- Two are getting fish and chips.
- The other sees a strange creature crawl into an empty shell.
- He tells the other two about this strange creature.
- One goes back to the fish and chip shop and brings back a poster telling of a competition to discover a new species of animal with a £10,000 prize.
- The three silly men try to get the creature out of the shell: ordering, shouting and finally shaking. The animal in the shell clings harder to the inside.
- Eventually the three men give up and walk away, leaving the shell behind.

- Gina, who has been watching, now picks up the shell, puts the last bit of her ice cream in front of it and then takes out her phone and prepares the camera.
- Quite soon the little creature pokes its head out of the shell and nibbles the ice cream cone.
- Gina takes lots of pictures and then sends them to the Natural History Museum to enter the competition.
- After a while Gina's family get a call to tell her that she has won £10,000.
- Gina says to the paper that if you want something or someone to do something it is better to be nice to them and make them feel safe.

# The Genius Glasses

Queen Ermintrude was a miserable queen. She was always cross, she rarely smiled and she never, ever – not once in anyone's memory – laughed out loud. Because she was the Queen and in charge, her being grumpy all the time made everyone in the palace grumpy, and that made everyone in the kingdom miserable as well. It was as though everyone had always just got bad news, every single day. If people visited from other places, they thought "What a miserable place," and left.

Over time, the kingdom became duller and duller. There were no bright colours, no smiley faces, no parties, no concerts, nothing which was fun. It was a gloomy place to live, and that's a fact. Even the birds stopped singing and the sun rarely seemed to shine.

One day, two teenagers were walking home from school.

"Aren't we unlucky to live in a kingdom which is the most miserable place in the world, ruled over by the most miserable queen," said one.

"Yeah," said the second, "I can't imagine what it's like to live in a happy place, where people are friendly and chatty and smile sometimes."

"No, me neither," agreed the first. "I wonder why it's such a miserable place?"

"Well, that's easy," the second said, with some volume, "it's down to the Queen. It's a well-known fact that if the person in charge is a misery, then everyone underneath them becomes a misery too."

"Is that right?" the first teenager questioned.

"Yeah, that's definitely the reason."

"So, if we could make the Queen happy, the entire kingdom would become happy?" the first teenager asked.

"Well, yes, that's right. But it's easy to say things like that. Have you ever seen the Queen look anywhere near happy? You are more likely to see a penguin fly than see Queen Ermintrude crack a smile."

"Yes, you're right. I guess we are stuck living in Grumpyland."

The teenagers continued their way home feeling fed up and very unlucky. If only they could change things!

That night, one of the teenagers was reading his little sister her favourite story, 'The Emperor's New Clothes', a story about two crooks who persuaded an Emperor that only clever people could see the cloth from which they had made a suit. The Emperor, because he didn't want people to think he was stupid, said that he could see it, but actually there was nothing there at all. The crooks were playing a trick, and the Emperor went on a walk through the streets in just his underpants. The story gave the teenager an idea, and that night he lay in his bed thinking through a plan.

The next day, he rushed up to his friend to tell him what he had been planning.

"It's all based on glasses," he excitedly said.

"What, are we going to give her a drink? Some happy juice or something?"

"No, not those glasses, the glasses that the Queen wears to see properly. I have had an idea about how we can get the Queen to be less grumpy." He was very excited because he thought his plan might actually work.

The two friends sat and talked through the plan. At first the one who hadn't thought of it thought his friend was bonkers, but slowly he started to think maybe it could work, but it would certainly be tricky.

Two days later, one of the teenagers, dressed in his dad's best suit, went to see if he could get to speak to the Queen. He had to pretend to be a brilliant person, a man called Professor Humperdink.

"Hello," he said to the guards at the castle entrance, "I am Professor Heinz Humperdink and I am a professor of genius studies at the University of Sinselburg. I would like to see the Queen."

The guards laughed (an unusual sight in the palace). "You can't just come here and ask to see the Queen. If we let you in, she'll go mad, even though she is in a pretty good mood for her. She's only shouted at us 6 times so far today, it's usually 10 by now."

"I see," said the teenager, still using his best 'Professor' voice. "Well, could you kindly pass on this card? It is most urgent, and the Queen will very much like what it says."

"I doubt that," said the guard, "she doesn't like much."

"Well, she will like this," said the 'Professor'. He turned and walked away, trying to think how professors walk and nearly falling over.

"I'll take it to her," said one of the guards. And to his great surprise, the Queen actually did like it. Not enough to make her smile on the outside, but enough to make her want to know more. The card said:

*"Your Majesty; I am Professor Heinz Humperdink from the University of Sinselburg. I am studying the great thinking minds of our world. I have developed a special device which can identify people who are geniuses. I believe that you might be such a genius. I would like the chance to examine you using my device. Please contact me on this phone number- 0567-12211-2 to arrange a meeting. There are very few people who are clever enough to pass this test, but I think you could well be one of them."*

The only thing which made the Queen even a bit happy was other people thinking she was clever, and she was fairly clever. So, she got one of her helpers to call the number and soon it was arranged. The Queen would meet with the 'Professor' two days later in the main town square – the 'Professor' had suggested this as a place to meet. As usual, the Queen was in a foul mood, complaining about the weather, the bumpy road and anything else that she could moan about. When the Queen's car arrived, the 'Professor' was waiting for her.

"Your Majesty," he said, "what an honour it is to meet you."

"Yes, it is," the Queen snapped. "OK, where is the machine?"

"It's here, Your Highness." The 'Professor' took a pair of glasses from his jacket pocket.

"Is that it? Is this a joke?" the grumpy Queen snapped at him.

"Yes, this is it! But it is no joke, Your Highness, no joke at all."

"But it's just a pair of glasses."

"Yes, but not an ordinary pair of glasses. These are very special spectacles, watch this."

He approached a stranger in the square. "Hello madam, would you mind putting on these glasses and telling me what you see?" He handed over the glasses.

The lady put them on and said, "I just see the same as I did before, there is no difference."

"Oh, for goodness' sake, what a waste of time. Come on!" the Queen ordered her guards.

"No, wait Your Majesty. That person was not clever enough to see anything different. These glasses only work for geniuses. Let's try another person."

This time he went up to his friend, who was pretending to just be part of the crowd. "Excuse me sir, would you mind trying these glasses?"

"OK," said the friend. He put the glasses on. "Wow!" He exclaimed. "Wow, that's incredible. I can just see lovely things. The blue sky seems bluer, the flowers are brighter, the pictures in that open-air gallery over there seem more beautiful. This is amazing, I feel so happy." Of course, it was all a trick, nothing had really changed; in fact, the glasses we just normal sunglasses. But by now, the Queen was very interested.

The Professor continued, "Ha, excellent! Could you tell me your name and job, please?"

"My name is Charles Einskens and I am Professor of Brilliance at the University of Goldenstone."

"Ah! You see, Your Majesty, this explains why this man could see the special effects of the glasses. Only those people who are geniuses can see this effect, other normal people cannot. This is why I wanted you to try the glasses, Your Highness, because I think that you are a genius."

"Oh, well yes. I think I should try them then. I am sure I am as clever as this man." The Queen said, she was a little anxious but keen to try.

She took the glasses (which were fake, remember) and put them on. They made no difference at all to what the Queen could see, but of course she did not want anyone to think she was not a genius, so she lied. "Oh," she said, "gosh, all the good things are so clear." She quickly looked for good things; she saw a little boy helping his mum, and a driver stop to let an old man cross the road. "Oh, look at those lovely people helping each other," she said. She actually felt quite good saying it. The glasses had changed nothing, but because she was looking for good things, she was finding them. The Queen sensed a strange feeling in her face, and suddenly she realised...she was smiling!

"As I thought," said the 'Professor', "you are a genius. Whenever you wear these glasses, you will see good things. Your Majesty, you may keep these glasses."

From that day on, the Queen would wear the glasses and because she was looking for good things, she found them. She smiled more and slowly the people of her kingdom learned how to smile again. The kingdom became a cheerful place because the Queen always looked for good things rather than bad things.

The two teenagers went back to school, knowing they had tricked the Queen, but that it had made her and the entire kingdom happier. Because they knew, if you look for the good things, you will usually find them.

# THE GENIUS GLASSES

In this story, a miserable and angry Queen is tricked into looking for good rather than bad by a couple of teenagers who want their kingdom to be a happier place. They are inspired by the 'Emperor's New Clothes' story and they make the place better for everyone.

The themes are:

- Miserable leaders make miserable people and places.
- If you look for positives, you will find them.
- Vanity makes you easy to trick.

### Story map

- Queen Ermintrude is a miserable woman, and this makes everyone around her miserable.
- The Queen is also someone who likes people to think that she is very clever.
- Two teenage friends don't like living in such a miserable place and feel they want to change things and feel that they must cheer the Queen up somehow.
- When reading the story of the 'Emperor's New Clothes' to his little sister, one of them has an idea.
- The two boys get a message to the Queen telling her that they believe that she is super clever, and they would like to test her using their special glasses.
- They meet the Queen and say that the glasses they have invented allow very clever people to see things in a better way.

- The first person who is a member of the public sees nothing different (of course).
- The second person (who is the other teenager) says he can see everything positively and see how wonderful things look. He then says he is a Professor of Brilliance.
- The Queen is the third person and wants to appear clever as well. She pretends to see things which are good and without really realising she experiences feeling happy and she smiles.

➢ From that day onwards the Queen wears the glasses regularly and because she is looking for good things she finds them, and slowly the country becomes a much happier place.

# The Unhappy Prince

Once, a long time ago, in a place which probably never existed, there lived a wise King. He was a good man and was loved by the people of his kingdom. The land had peace, and everyone had enough to eat. The King would look out of his palace window, across his land, and feel content. His wife, the Queen, had died many years earlier and although he still missed her, he had realised that while wonderful memories were precious and special, it was important to look forward and to be grateful for what you have in life. He also realised that he was very, very lucky to be the King. Every day, he looked in the mirror and said, "George," because that was his name, "you're a lucky man, remember it." And whatever had happened during the day, he would always remember that he was a lucky man to have all that he had. Even when things went wrong or when he had problems, he always thought, despite all the trouble, he was a lucky, lucky man.

Prince Hubert, on the other hand, was not a cheerful man. He was constantly glum and always felt that things were against him. He felt that things went wrong for him when they would go right for other people. He often said things like, "just my luck," and, "that's typical of my life," and, "well of course it's gone wrong, everything which is mine goes wrong." He was always miserable and because of this, the people around him were miserable. Even though he was a prince, nobody really wanted to spend time with him and of course this made Hubert even gloomier.

One day, King George was in his study looking at important king stuff. He was unusually quiet because the harvest had not been good, and it worried him that the people of the kingdom might not have enough to eat when the winter came. Although he was worried, he said to himself that he had to think clearly and not get miserable. "I'm a very lucky man and we will sort this out."

He worked hard all morning, planning how the kingdom could have enough food to survive. By 11:50 am he had everything sorted. He had managed to get food from his friend, Queen Alice, in the next kingdom and all would be OK. Just as the King was sitting back, feeling relieved and fairly pleased with himself, Hubert walked in, looking glum, of course.

"Oh Dad, you'll never guess what has happened, I can't believe it, it's a nightmare!" the prince moaned.

"Oh, is it really Hubert?" the King asked, wishing his son wasn't so miserable all the time, "What has happened now?"

"Oh honestly, Father, I can hardly tell you. I have had these new shoes made by the best shoemaker in the whole of Italy. I had them brought all the way here, and they are absolutely beautiful. But the first time I wore them, I scratched them on a nail which was sticking out of a door in the kitchen. I just can't believe it!" He shouted the last bit, stamped his feet and stormed off.

The King felt sorry for Hubert, but also thought it was not really a huge problem. He had spent the morning thinking about whether there would be enough food to feed the people of the kingdom, and Hubert was just bothered about his new shoes.

The King pondered for a long time. He knew that one day Hubert would be the king, and he thought he had to find a way to stop his son from feeling sorry for himself and help him to realise that he was actually very, very lucky and had a lot to be grateful for.

The King was still thinking about it the next day when Madelina, his most trusted adviser, came into his office. "Are you OK, Your Majesty?" she asked. "It's not like you to look troubled."

"Oh, I worry about very little, but I do worry about Hubert. He is going to be the king one day and all he sees is bad luck and trouble. I wish I could find a way to make him see all the good things he has. He always thinks life is against him, but he is so lucky." The King talked at some length, and Madelina sat and listened.

She waited until he had stopped speaking and then said, "Hubert has had such a privileged life. He does not realise how some people have real problems. Problems which really make their lives very difficult. If we could help him realise that the life he has is good, then he might appreciate it and understand the problems other people have. That will make him a better king when his time comes." Madelina knew the King didn't mind her talking like that, but she still felt a bit embarrassed.

"Yes, exactly," said the King, "but how do we help him see these things?"

Madelina thought and then said, "I have an idea, Your Majesty. Am I allowed to do whatever it takes?"

"Well, as long as you don't hurt him badly, yes of course."

"And you will back me up when he complains to you?" the adviser asked.

"If it helps him be a better king one day, then yes, certainly I will." The King was curious about what Madelina had in mind, but he knew she was still thinking about her plan, and he would have to wait a while.

"Can you get Hubert to the stables tomorrow at midday, Your Majesty?" she eventually asked.

"Yes, of course." The King was quite excited. "I shall make sure he is there."

The next day, Hubert was not happy about being told he had to be at the stables at midday. "Oh, it's just my luck to go there when it's pouring down with rain," he moaned.

"There are just a few spots of rain, Hubert," his father said, "hardly anything at all."

"I can't believe I have to go to a stinky stable when there isn't even a race, or we aren't even going for a ride. Oh, I hate my life so much!" the prince complained.

"You have a lucky life, Hubert, "the King said sadly, "I wish you could see that."

"Well, why do I have to go to the muddy stables if my life is so great?" the stroppy prince asked.

"I'm not sure," said the King, "let's go and find out."

When they arrived at the stables, Madelina was already there, and she was smiling. Hubert didn't like Madelina. She was clever, and she thought he was spoilt. She also could tell the King what to do.

"Hello, Your Majesty, Your Highness," she greeted the royal pair.

"Good afternoon, Madelina. Are things ready?" the King asked, even though he didn't know what the 'things' were.

Hubert did not like the sound of this. Madelina stamped her feet twice and two big, strong stable hands came out and grabbed hold of Hubert. "What's going on?" he shouted, "Father, these people are attacking me. Help!"

"It will be fine," said the King, a little worried, but he had told Madelina that he would support her plan.

A third, very strong looking stable hand entered with a rucksack. It looked extremely heavy, even in the powerful arms of the stable hand. She placed the rucksack over Hubert's shoulders until it sat on his back as if he were going camping. But when the stable hand let go, Hubert fell to the floor under its weight.

"Urgghhh!" Hubert cried. "What's happening father?"

"I'm not sure," said the King, "Madelina, can you tell us?"

"Of course, Your Majesty. The stable hands have locked a rucksack full of rocks to Hubert's back, and he will have to wear it for one week. That's all," she said with a smile.

"I'm not wearing this for a week. I can hardly stand. Father, this woman has lost her mind. Have her thrown in jail."

The King remembered his promise to Madelina,

"No Hubert, I shall not have her thrown in jail, and you shall wear the rucksack for a week."

"But how can I change my clothes and take a bath and visit friends and go to parties and do all the other things I like?" said Hubert.

"Well maybe you cannot, Your Highness," said Madelina, and she left.

The King also departed, leaving Hubert staggering to his feet. He tried to take off the rucksack, but he could not. Eventually he staggered back towards the palace; slowly and uncomfortably he got to his room.

He did not sleep well that night. The rucksack was lumpy, and the straps rubbed on his shoulders. The next morning, he went downstairs for breakfast. The King smiled to himself on seeing his son. He knew it would not be a good day for him. He knew Hubert would moan... and he did. "I cannot believe you have let that mad woman do this to me. I hardly slept, I ache all over and the straps have rubbed my skin so it's all red. Have you gone crazy, Father, to let that woman do this to me?"

"No, Hubert, I have not gone crazy," said the King, and he left for his office.

That day, Hubert tried to go hunting with some of his rich friends, but he couldn't get on the horse with the heavy rucksack.

Again, that night, he didn't sleep well. He was very unhappy. More unhappy than he had ever been.

For Hubert, the days seemed to go on forever. Each was full of pain and disappointments at not being able to do the things he enjoyed, with the people he liked. As the week went on, Hubert became more miserable, and the King felt terrible for making his son so unhappy. He asked Madelina if she was sure that this was the right thing to do, but she said she was, so he said no more.

By the end of the seventh day, Hubert was so tired and so miserable that he hardly spoke. The King and Madelina asked him to come to the office. He arrived, of course carrying the big rucksack full of rocks on his back. He was dirty and his clothes looked a mess. They were the same clothes he had worn all week.

The King signalled to Madelina, and she spoke. "Prince Hubert, I am sorry that you have had such an awful week, but I wanted you to understand that some people carry problems with them all the time. Some don't have enough to eat, some cannot walk well, some don't have a change of clothes or a place to wash. Some work so hard that they are always tired or even injured. You have had a tough week, but those people have difficult lives. I hope the last seven days have helped you to realise what a lucky life you have, and how some things you complain about are not really that important."

At this point the stable hands arrived and unlocked the rucksack and took it away. Hubert let out a sigh of relief and stretched his sore back. He had not understood why he had been made to wear the heavy rucksack, but now he did. He was still angry, and he left the office without speaking.

However, from that day he didn't moan about silly things which didn't really matter, and he understood the hardships of less fortunate people, and you know what? He was actually a much happier Prince, and would, when it was his time, make a much better King.

# THE UNHAPPY PRINCE

This is a story about a lucky, rich prince who too readily feels sorry for himself. He thinks the world is against him and does not realise that other people have much more serious problems and difficult lives.

The themes are:

- Being grateful for what you have.
- Appreciating other people's situations.
- Learning from experience.

## Story map

- King George is a good man and a good king who thinks that he is lucky, and he cares for the people of his land.
- Prince Hubert is a miserable young man who thinks that everything is against him.
- The King works hard every day to make the people of the nation safe and happy.
- King George worries about his son and wishes he was more appreciative.
- The King's adviser Madelina notices that the King is unhappy and asks him what is wrong. The King tells her of his worries.
- Madelina says that she has an idea and asks if the King will back her; he says he will.
- Hubert is told to meet the King and Madelina at the stables. He is not happy about getting muddy. There,

- some stable hands lock a bag of rocks to his back. He is not at all happy.
- Madelina tells Hubert that he will have to wear the sack of rocks for the whole week. He is furious.
- At first, Hubert shouts and screams but then has to get on with life. He cannot ride his horses, party with his friends, or even sleep in his big comfy bed.
- The prince has a terrible week and is very cross with his father and Madelina and tells them so.
- Madelina says that it has all been her doing but she wanted the prince to know what it was like to carry a real burden all day every day. Some people carried the burden of poor health, hunger or poverty around with them all day every day for their entire lives.
- The prince remains angry but slowly the message sinks in and he starts to appreciate his life and is a better and happier prince.

# Trouble with the Birds and the Beasts

There had been trouble between the birds and the beasts for as long as anyone could remember. No one really knew why or what had started the trouble, but they just didn't get along. The birds thought they were the best because they could fly and were brightly coloured, and the beasts (who were mammals really) thought that they were the best because they were often bigger and stronger; they thought birds were stupid and show-offs for the way some of them flashed their colourful feathers around.

One wild and stormy night, a bat was flying home when she got caught in the powerful wind. She was blown this way and that way. She fought hard to keep going, to find her way home, but she was just not strong enough and eventually, exhausted, she landed on the wide branch of a twisted old oak tree. She was a soggy, wet mess. Her chest was heaving up and down as she tried to get her breath back. She was so tired she could hardly lift her head. The wide branches of the tree gave some shelter, and many birds were using it as a place to sit out the storm.

Suddenly she heard a friendly voice. "Hello."

She raised her head and said, "hello."

She could see that she was being spoken to by a blackbird. It was difficult to see him in the dark, only the glassy glint of his eyes and the shine on his beak could really be seen in the faint moonlight. "I haven't seen you round here before. Where have you come from?" As the blackbird said this, some other birds, who were curious to see what was happening and who the stranger was, joined them.

"No," said the bat, still panting, "I don't think I have ever been here before. To be honest, I don't really know where I am. I was flying home, and the storm has blown me off course."

"Oh, you poor thing," said one bird who had landed nearby. Another bird dropped some worms in front of the bat. "Here, have some of these, you have had a terrible time." The bat thanked the bird and ate the worms. They tasted good, and she was really grateful.

"I suppose being blown about is one problem with being able to fly. Haha, I bet those stupid beasts would like to have that problem. At least us birds can fly up into big trees like this and shelter from the storm and get off the soaking ground. The beasts are down there stuck in the mud and soaking wet, haha," said the blackbird, laughing. The other birds all laughed and made fun of the beasts. The bat felt uncomfortable knowing that she was a mammal, and so was a beast in their eyes. But the birds, who thought of the bat as a bird, because she could fly, were nice to her. She was still exhausted and so she stayed quiet as the birds all chatted and made fun of the beasts.

The bat woke up with the sunrise and saw that the storm had passed. Most of the birds were up and many were flying around looking for something to eat for breakfast.

"How are you feeling today?" a sparrow asked.

"I'm OK, thanks. Thank you for being so nice to me last night, you were all really kind."

"Well, you're one of us, aren't you? Us birds have got to stick together," a magpie said.

"Er... well, I suppose so," the bat said, uncomfortably.

"If you don't mind me saying," the sparrow continued, "You are a strange-looking bird."

"Oh," said the bat, "what do you mean?" She knew exactly what the sparrow meant.

"Well, your feathers, they're more like fur and you don't really have a beak."

Another sparrow had heard and flew nearer. "You know I was thinking just that. Your wings are skin rather than feathered like ours."

"Oh, well, it's just how I am," said the bat, and as she spoke the sparrows became very loud.

"Oh wow, you have teeth. I didn't see them before, but you have teeth," the magpie joined in.

"No bird has teeth. You're not a bird at all!" the second sparrow shouted. "You are a beast, not a bird."

The birds completely changed their attitude. Rather than being the kind, welcoming creatures they had been the night before, they were suddenly angry and aggressive.

"Well, yes, I am a bat, a flying mammal so I guess I am a beast, but I'm just the same as I was last night."

"No, you are not. You're a mammal, a beast — you're not one of us." The birds were now very angry and aggressive. Other birds had heard the fuss and flocked towards them.

"She's a spy, they sent her here to see what we were doing," the magpie said excitedly.

"No, no, I'm not. I got blown here by the storm, like I said," the bat pleaded.

"She is not one of us," shouted a thrush, "get her!" With that, the birds jumped at the bat who flew off out of the tree.

Although bats can fly well, they cannot fly as well as most birds. Soon the birds were swooping at her as she tried to get away. They were pecking at her and hitting her with their claws. The bat was being badly beaten and eventually fell out of the sky. The birds swooped down, but luckily the bat fell near a crack in a rock and she managed to squeeze into it. The birds landed and tried to keep attacking the poor bat, but they couldn't reach her with their beaks. The bat was terrified. Eventually, the birds got bored and flew away.

After a while, the frightened bat crawled out of the crack and looked around.

"Oi, are you OK?" It was a squirrel. "What's happened to you?"

"A gang of birds chased me. It was horrible," the terrified bat managed to say.

"Well, what do you expect from birds? They are stupid animals, all of them."

A rabbit arrived. "I haven't seen you around here before. What's the matter?"

"The birds," said the squirrel, "they chased her. Sounds bad."

"Oh, I really don't like the birds, none of them. They are all horrible," said the rabbit.

"Yeah!" said a fox who was passing, "those stupid birds."

"Well, they were nice to me at first," said the bat.

"Don't defend them," said the rabbit, "they attacked you."

"Yes, I suppose so," the bat admitted.

The animals talked for a long time until, eventually, the bat felt tired and wanted to sleep. She said thank you to the animals for their company, but she was going to sleep, and without thinking she flew up into the tree to sleep. The animals looked at one another. They had not seen the bat's wings since they had been folded up at her side.

"Did you see that?" said the fox.

"I did. She flew into the tree; flew I tell ya!" The squirrel was very excited, and his tail fluffed up.

"Well, we know what animals fly, don't we?" the fox added.

"We do," said the rabbit.

"Oi," called the fox. "Could you come down here?"

The bat again didn't think too hard and flew down to the ground. As soon as the bat touched the floor the animals grabbed her.

"Ha, we got you. Do you think we're stupid? You come here and pretend to be one of us and then fly into the tree. We know what you are! You're a bird, eh, aren't you?" They went to drag the bat away, but luckily she managed to wriggle free and fly back up into the tree's branches.

"I'm honestly not a bird. I'm a bat, a flying mammal," the poor bat shouted down.

The fox was jumping up at the tree trunk, and more alarmingly still, the squirrel had started to climb the tree and was shouting nasty things. The squirrel, who had been lovely so far, was now being horrible.

The bat thought this was dreadful and flew away before the squirrel could reach her. She flew around for a while, trying to find her way back home. Eventually, she spotted a rock face that she recognised, and then, at last, the cave where she and her friends lived.

Her friends were thrilled to see her. They flew round her to ask where she had been. She told her friends of her adventure and how she had been attacked by the birds because she was a mammal, and by the mammals who thought she was a bird.

Her friends couldn't understand and told her how terrible they thought this all was.

"Oh, it must have been dreadful," said one of the other bats.

"You poor thing, I bet you wish you had never gone out," said another.

"Well, yes, in a way. But it's good to learn things, and I have learned that creatures can change how they treat you based on their own prejudice, not on how you are as an individual. If they have hatred in their hearts, it can make them behave in a way that they would not otherwise. I have learned that we should all try to see others for who they are, not which group they belong to."

# TROUBLE WITH THE BIRDS AND THE BEASTS

A bat gets blown off course and is treated differently by groups depending on if they think she is a bird or a beast. The bat learns an important lesson about judging others.

The themes are:

- It is foolish to judge people or things by which group they belong to.
- Individuals act differently when a group puts pressure on each other.
- It is better to judge by who someone is rather than who we think they are.

## Story map

- ➢ There has always been trouble between the birds and the beasts (mammals).
- ➢ They mock each other and each thinks they are superior.
- ➢ One stormy night a young bat gets blown off course and shelters in a tree.
- ➢ The birds, thinking that she is a bird, are kind and caring.
- ➢ When the morning comes the birds realise that she is not actually a bird and attack and chase her. She manages to squeeze behind a rock to escape.

- Some forest mammals find her and help her. They are mean about the birds.
- The bat flies up into a tree and the beasts who had helped her now think that she is a bird, because she can fly. They try to attack her. Again, she manages to escape.
- Eventually the bat finds her way home and tells her friends of her frightening adventure.
- When her friends say that she must regret going out, she tells them that whilst it was a horrible experience, she has really learned that it is much more important to judge someone by who they are rather than what they are or which group they belong to.

# **Three Farmers**

Once, there were three sisters. They were very different from one another. Susan was hard-working and knew what she wanted. She thought people should only have what they deserved. Sharon was a kind, thoughtful person who wanted to help everyone, and Catherine was a fun-loving person who could be lazy at times but had a good heart.

As they were growing up, they were like most sisters and brothers, in that they got along most of the time, but sometimes they argued and rowed. However, generally things were good between them, and they loved each other.

Again, like most brothers and sisters, they were quite competitive, whether it be a card game, or playing at the beach. They wanted to beat one another, but they also liked it when one of their sisters did well at something.

The sisters' mother was a farmer who owned the big successful farm where they grew up. One day, the girls were called to come and see their mum.

When they arrived, she was sitting at the large wooden table in the dining room. She was a small, strong woman who had the look of someone who had spent most of her life outside. She clearly had something very important to say.

"I am tired of the cold, early mornings, and the hard work of the farm. I have worked for 40 years building this farm and now it is the biggest and best farm in the entire county. Now it is time for me to have some fun. I have saved enough money to live in

Spain, where it will be warm, and I can relax and have some fun as I grow old. I have drawn up a plan."

She rolled out a large map of the farm that filled the entire table. "I have divided the farm into three equal parts. Each has good growing land, and each has a building on it, which you can turn into a delightful house. Each part also has water and roads in and out. I have made my one wonderful farm into three smaller, but still wonderful farms. I shall give you each a third of the animals and enough seed to grow crops for the first growing season."

The sisters were shocked. They had not expected this and didn't know what to do. They looked at one another and realised that their mother had worked incredibly hard on the farm and deserved to have some time to enjoy life. They looked at the map and each liked the part of the farm which they had been given.

"Good," said Susan, "my land has the big field. I can really work hard there and grow lots of crops. I shall make lots of money and have plenty to eat."

"Oh good," said Sharon, "my land is near the best pasture. I can put ponies on there, so that the children from the town can come ride and have some fun."

"Excellent," said Catherine, "my land is nearest the town, I shall not have far to walk if I want to go out to see my friends."

So, each sister was pleased with the farmland they had been given, and soon the day came for their mother to move away to enjoy the sunshine and swim in the Mediterranean Sea. They took her to the airport and waved her goodbye.

Straight away they all got to work. They worked hard, and things were going well. As expected, Susan, the hardest working sister, worked tirelessly. She spent long hours every day in the fields and did not even take a day off for her birthday. Sharon worked hard as well but spent some of her time teaching the town's children to ride the ponies. And Catherine worked quite hard but made sure she could see her friends and visit their mother sometimes.

Things were good for the first two years. The crops grew well. Susan had the largest harvests, then Sharon and then Catherine. But they all had enough, and each of them was happy; Susan enjoyed hard work, Sharon enjoyed helping people, especially the children at her riding school, and Catherine was still having a fun time and she loved visiting Spain to see her mum.

Then, during the third year, things were not as good. There was hardly any rain, and the harvest was poor. Susan, the hard-working sister, was fine because she had dug some wells and had enough water for her crops. Susan's harvest was not as good as it had been but was still good enough. Sharon was just about OK as well because her farm was by the river, and she had dug ditches to hold water for her crops. However, Catherine had not dug ditches or wells; her fields were parched, and her crops did not grow.

Catherine had hardly any crops to harvest and asked to meet her sisters. "I have no food and no grain to sell. I cannot run my farm if I cannot buy new seed for the land and cannot feed my animals."

Sharon felt sorry for her sister. "Well, none of us have very much this year, it has been a very hard year. But I think if we put what we have together and then share it out, we shall all have enough."

"Oh, thank you!" said Catherine, looking at her kind sister.

"Why?" asked Susan.

"What do you mean 'Why?'" Sharon said, "our sister needs our help, and we can give it to her."

"Why should we help her? I spent hours and hours working, until my hands were bleeding, digging wells which have given me and my farm enough water. You have been lucky but still had to dig ditches to make sure that there was enough water for the fields. And where has Catherine been during the time we have been working? She has been with her friends having fun, or on the beach in Spain, with our mother. Why should we give her what we have worked so hard to make?"

"Because we can," said Sharon. "We can help our sister and we should. Better that we are all a bit hungry than one of us be starving."

"Well, our mother built this farm on hard work, she didn't go out much, or go on holidays. She worked as I have done, and I will not give it away." With that, Susan stormed off.

Catherine looked at Sharon and said, "She is right. You have both worked really hard to make your farms successful and I have had breaks and holidays, and rather than going to see Mum, I could have been working hard like you two. Maybe I don't deserve to be helped."

"Well, it's not about you! It's about what I can do and what I want to do. I can help you and I want to help you, so I shall help you."

Sharon shared her food and her seed with Catherine, and as it was a hard winter, sometimes they were both hungry. Susan was angry and felt that her sisters were against her. They were both struggling, and she had more than enough food, but she would not give in. She still wondered why Catherine should have holidays whilst she was working.

Things became difficult between the sisters, but the next year the farming was better. The crops grew well, and once again, all had enough to eat. Then, one hot sunny day, a fire took light in the forest around the sisters' farms. It was very close to Susan's enormous field, which was full of beautiful wheat and corn. It was near to the time when it would be harvested.

A small piece of burning wood blew onto the field and set the crops alight. The entire crop quickly caught fire, and before anyone could do anything, Susan's wheat and corn were gone – all of it. By the time Catherine and Sharon got there, Susan was slumped at the edge of her blackened, smouldering field, her head looking down at the scorched earth.

"I'm finished, I have nothing. All my hard work has gone." She could not look at her sisters.

Catherine spoke. "It's gone, but this does not finish you. We have enough grain for all of us. We can all work extra hard to get your field sorted out to be ready for planting, and we will have you up and growing again for next year. You'll see."

'Yes," said Sharon, "we will help you, please don't worry."

Susan looked at her sisters with smoky tears in her eyes. "Why?" she asked. "Why would you help me? I let you both go hungry this winter because I was jealous that Catherine had gone on holidays. I had plenty to eat, and you both went hungry. Why would you help me?"

Catherine looked at Sharon and smiled. She then looked at Susan and said, "It's not about you! It's about what we can do and what we want to do. We can help you and we want to help you, so we shall help you."

Susan looked at her sisters and understood what they meant. She had let how Catherine had behaved determine how she behaved. Because she was cross with Catherine, she had acted meanly to her. When her sisters were entitled to be angry with her, they were not, and they still did what their heart told them they should. Susan had learned an important lesson.

# **THREE FARMERS**

Three farming sisters, who are all different, inherit a farm from their mother. The hardest working sister learns that because she was angry with one of her sisters, she let that change the way she behaved, and that is not a good thing.

The themes are:

- Working together is important.
- Anger can make us behave poorly.
- Don't let the way others behave change how you behave.
- Helping others is a good thing to do.
- Forgiveness is an important quality.

## Story map

- Three sisters grow up on a huge and successful farm which their mother has built.
- One day the mother tells her three daughters that she has decided to retire to Spain.
- She divides the big farm into three smaller farms.
- Susan is the hardest-working, and feels you only get what you deserve.
- Sharon is hard-working but kind and caring.
- Catherine works fairly hard but likes to have fun and spend time with her friends.
- After two good years, in the third year there is little rain. Susan and Sharon have dug wells and ditches to hold

water, but Catherine has been away visiting their mother and friends and her crops fail.
- Sharon wants them all to share so that Catherine has enough to eat and has seeds to plant for the following year. Susan feels that Catherine deserves no help as she has not worked as hard.
- Susan shares her food and seed, but she and Catherine are hungry during the long winter, and it is a struggle.
- The following year the growing is good.
- Just before harvest time a fire burns all of Susan's crops. She feels she is ruined.
- Her sisters tell her they will help her.
- Susan feels ashamed that she let her sisters go hungry and now they are willing to help her. She learns the lesson of not letting your anger make you behave in a way that you would not otherwise act.

# **Contact Chris**

I hope that you have enjoyed using these stories to make great assemblies. If you have any comments about any of the stories, or assemblies in general, please feel free to contact me. If you are a film producer who would like to make one of the stories into a blockbuster, that's fine, we can talk!

I am currently working on a second volume of assembly stories:

**Keeping Them Awake!**

**Chrispearsoneducation@outlook.com**

Thanks,

Chris

Printed in Great Britain
by Amazon